Fifty ways to improve your

Intercultural Skills in English

Bob Dignen with James Chamberlain

Summertown
Publishing

HEINLE
CENGAGE Learning™

Australia • Brazil • Japan • Korea • Mexico • Singapore • Spain • United Kingdom • United States

HEINLE
CENGAGE Learning

50 Ways to Improve Your Intercultural Skills
Bob Dignen and James Chamberlain

Publisher: Nick Sheard

Manufacturing Team Lead: Paul Herbert

Production Controller: Tom Relf

Head of Inventory: Jane Glendening

Typesetter: Oxford Designers & Illustrators

Cover Design: Oxford Designers & Illustrators

For product information and technology assistance,
contact **emea.info@cengage.com**.

For permission to use material from this text or product,
and for permission queries,
email **clsuk.permissions@cengage.com**.

ISBN: 978-1-902741-85-7

Cengage Learning EMEA

Cheriton House, North Way, Andover, Hampshire, SP10 5BE, United Kingdom

Cengage Learning is a leading provider of customised learning solutions with office locations around the globe, including Singapore, the United Kingdom, Australia, Mexico, Brazil and Japan. Locate our local office at **international.cengage.com/region**

Cengage Learning products are represented in Canada by Nelson Education Ltd.

Visit Heinle online at **http://elt.heinle.com**
Visit our corporate website at **www.cengage.com**

Acknowledgements
The authors would like to thank the editors, Will Capel and Sally Cooke, for their helpful, clear and analytical approach, Louis Garnade and the rest of the Summertown Publishing team, and the ODI design team.

The authors and the publishers would like to acknowledge the following sources of material used in this book: WorldWork (www.worldwork.biz): *International Profiler* (see pp.9–10; p.101, pp.133–5). Addison Wesley, NY: Iceberg model, from *Beyond Language: Cross-cultural Communication* by Deena Levine and Mara Edelman, 1993 (see p.13). Cassell Publishing: Onion model, from *Culturally Speaking: Culture, Communication and Politeness* by Helen Spencer-Oatley, 2000 (see p.14). Nicholas Brealey Publishing Ltd: Mole map, from *Mind Your Manners: Managing Business Cultures in Europe* by John Mole, Revised edn, 1995 (see p.23); dialogues, from *The Art of Crossing Cultures* by Craig Storti, 1990 (see p.43). Intercultural Press: Opinions/values cards, from *Developing Intercultural Awareness: A Crosscultural Training Handbook* by L. Robert Kohls and John M. Knight, 1994 (see p.29); intercultural flowcharts, from *The Art of Crossing Cultures* by Craig Storti, 1990 (see pp.33–4). HarperCollins, NY: Summary of six principles of persuasion, from *Influence* by Robert Cialdini, © Robert Cialdini 1993, reprinted by permission of HarperCollins Publishers William Morrow (see pp.64–5). McGraw-Hill: Negotiation principles, from *Negotiation: Readings, Exercises and Cases* by Roy Lewicki, 2003 (see pp.95–6). Canadian Foreign Institute: Profiler (www.dfaitmaeci. gc.ca/cfsi-icse/cil-cai/home-en.asp) (see p.100). Pearson Education, NJ: Leadership model, from *Management of Organizational Behavior* by P. Hersey, K. Blanchard and D. Johnson, 9th edn, 2008 (see p.125).

Printed by Zrinski D.D., Croatia
2 3 4 5 6 7 8 9 10 – 12 11 10

Foreword

Do you want to learn how to communicate more effectively across cultures?

Do you want to feel more confident when working with people from other cultures?

Do you want to understand some of the major differences between cultures which make collaboration in business more challenging?

Do you want some ideas on how to work more effectively in international teams and how to improve your international leadership skills?

If the answer to any of these questions is *Yes* then this is the book for you!

This is a self-help manual for those business people:

– who have English as their second language

– who use English to communicate with people from different cultures

– who want to develop their intercultural competence and international effectiveness.

You can use this book in several ways:

- You can use it regularly as a manual to help you prepare for working across cultures.
- You can read it from cover to cover as part of a self-development programme to improve all areas of your intercultural competence.
- You can use it as part of a wider programme to support international effectiveness in your team or organisation.
- You can give this book as a present to someone you know will benefit from it (and borrow it back if you need to!).

You can use this book in a variety of ways. Everybody has a preferred learning style and this book is flexible enough to meet yours. It is designed to be practical and to give you a lot of ideas about culture and its relationship to international business. The key words are *flexibility* and *usefulness*.

If you have read this foreword without too much difficulty, you are at the right language level to benefit from this book.

We would welcome any feedback on your use of this book. You can email us at info@summertown.co.uk if you have any comments.

Good luck!

Bob Dignen   James Chamberlain

Contents

5

Other titles in this series:

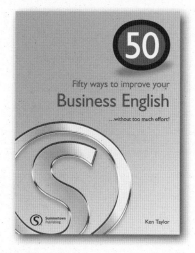

Introduction

'Of course, you have to realise that culture is a construct. When I have intelligent students in my class, I tell them, "One thing we have to agree on: culture does not exist." Culture is a concept that we made up which helps us understand a complex world, but it is not something tangible like a table or a human being.'   Geert Hofstede

Fifty Ways to Improve Your Intercultural Skills in English is designed to give you a greater understanding of the term *culture* and what it means for working internationally.

This book and accompanying **audio CD** will make you more sensitive to key dimensions of cultural diversity, for example differing concepts of time and leadership.

You will also become more aware of yourself – your own values, attitudes and behaviours, and how these impact on other people.

Importantly, the book will give you ideas on how to manage diversity with listening and speaking techniques which will help you to build common understanding.

The 50 units are divided into ten modules:

- Module 1 looks at dimensions of cultural diversity
- Modules 2 focuses on how we can understand ourselves
- Modules 3 and 4 examine skills for listening effectively and speaking clearly across cultures
- Modules 5 and 6 deal with intercultural issues when presenting, participating in meetings, negotiating, telephoning and writing emails
- Module 7 looks at strategies for building better relationships across cultures
- Module 8 provides ideas on how to work more effectively in international teams
- Module 9 gives ideas on how to be a better international leader
- Module 10 provides a summary of language to manage five key communication skills for those working internationally – building relationships, influencing, taking decisions, managing conflict and coaching.

The dialogues and short presentations on the audio CD give you the opportunity to develop your intercultural skills by listening to different communication styles and analysing their effectiveness.

By hearing the impact of speaking and listening in different ways during meetings and social conversations, you will become more sensitive to the motivation of the people talking to you in your workplace, and how individuals across cultures can interpret what you say in very different ways.

In each unit you are asked to transfer the main ideas to your own international working context – to think about how to build common understanding and more effective working relationships.

On the next two pages is an introduction to key **intercultural competences** which you can use to profile your own international working style. This will also help you identify which modules and units to focus on.

Profiling your international working style

In this section you can profile your international working style by analysing your own thinking and behaviours across ten intercultural attitudes and behaviours*.

Read the descriptions below and tick *Yes*, *No* or *It depends* if they describe your general international working style or not. Then read the summary on pages 151–2 to find out the meaning of your scores and ideas for personal development.

Remember, there are no 'right' answers – it isn't necessary to mark *Yes* to all the descriptions below. The important thing when working internationally is to know your own style, to observe the styles of others and then *do something* to manage any differences between the styles positively.

Profiling your international working style

1 Meeting new people	
I like to be the one who makes the first contact and builds relationships with new people, especially those who have different experiences and values from my own. I take a strong interest in people from different and unfamiliar cultural backgrounds.	Yes / No / It depends
2 Being flexible	
I adapt easily to a range of different social and cultural situations. I have learned, or I want to learn, a wide range of behaviours. I am ready to experiment with different ways of behaving to find those that are most acceptable for others.	Yes / No / It depends
3 Focusing on objectives	
I set clear goals and tasks, and work with determination to achieve them, regardless of problems or pressures to compromise. I believe I can control much of my own destiny, and can make things happen in the world.	Yes / No / It depends
4 Dealing with change	
I look for variety, change and stimulation in life, and avoid safe and predictable environments. I push myself into uncomfortable and ambiguous situations, even if I am unsure that I have the skills required to be successful.	Yes / No / It depends

---

* This questionnaire derives from a set of intercultural competences developed by WorldWork for their *International Profiler*, a tool for developing intercultural competence in professionals working internationally.

5 Understanding how others see me	
I am aware of how I come across to others. I am sensitive to how I communicate, and how my behaviour is interpreted by international partners.	Yes / No / It depends

6 Listening effectively	
I check and clarify, rather than assume that I understand what people are saying. I do this by paraphrasing and exploring the words that they use and the meaning they attach to them.	Yes / No / It depends

7 Speaking clearly	
I am able to get my ideas across in an international context by communicating clearly. I explain my ideas with simple words, and I also make clear the positive motivation behind my ideas.	Yes / No / It depends

8 Understanding cultures	
I am interested in unfamiliar cultures, and I take time to learn about them. I use different strategies for gathering information, for example asking colleagues and clients about their culture, so that I can understand the cultural contexts I work in.	Yes / No / It depends

9 Influencing decisions	
I am good at understanding where political power lies in an organisation. I work hard to understand the different cultural contexts in which decisions are made.	Yes / No / It depends

10 Managing diversity	
I make sure that different cultural perspectives are properly understood and used in international teams and in the problem-solving process.	Yes / No / It depends

Understanding culture

Interculturally-effective persons have an understanding of the concept of culture and the influence it will have on their life and work abroad.

Centre for Intercultural Learning, Canadian Foreign Service Institute

Working across cultures creates many challenges for today's international professional. Not only is there more travel and longer periods of time spent abroad, but also globalisation is radically changing the ways people have to do business and how companies are organised.

Change can bring conflict, and communicating effectively in this changing world requires new skills to get your message across to colleagues, partners and clients.

The Centre for Intercultural Training at the Canadian Foreign Service Institute has defined a set of core competences required to be effective internationally. This first module in the book deals with one of those core competences – understanding the concept of culture.

The five units of this module will help you to understand what we mean by the concept of culture. We will focus on the ways in which national cultures have been classified and compared by various researchers. In the final unit we will move beyond descriptions of national cultures to look at a model for analysing corporate culture.

1 What is culture?

2 Dimensions of national culture – 1

3 Dimensions of national culture – 2

4 Culture and values

5 Understanding corporate culture

1 What is culture?

Think about the word *culture* for a moment and what it means for your professional life. What is the first thing you think of when you hear this word? Take a moment to write down everything that you associate with the word *culture* in the box below.

> *Culture is …*

You have probably written a long and varied list. Some people start by listing everyday things such as dress, food, language or how people greet each other, or behaviours that you notice as different when you arrive in another country to do business.

There may also be things on your list that are not so visible, such as rules, traditions or attitudes. Some people think of culture in terms of the arts, away from the world of business: music, theatre, art galleries, opera. This is sometimes referred to as 'Culture with a capital C' or 'high culture'.

When anthropologists talk about culture, they make a difference between **explicit culture**, things that can be seen, heard or felt – and **implicit culture**, things that are not so obvious, or even invisible. Put the ideas and examples about culture you listed above into the two categories below, depending on how easily they can be observed.

Visible	Invisible
dress, food, …	*rules, attitudes, …*

Models of culture

Anthropologists define culture as anything created by human beings. In business this means, for example, buildings, rules for meetings, traditions, attitudes to leadership – anything which is not the natural world. You could say that nature is what people work with to create culture: the raw material of culture.

If culture is indeed everything that is made by human beings, it becomes a little difficult to know what we mean by the word. Because of this, interculturalists often use models or metaphors to explain what they mean by culture. Here are three models.

The Iceberg model

This model shows that culture is both visible and invisible, and that most of it is invisible. The key to doing successful business in intercultural situations is:

1 Understand that there are many invisible factors which drive communication behaviour

2 Be prepared to deal with these factors before they suddenly become visible through conflict.

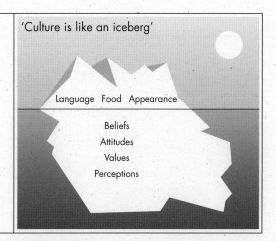

'Culture is like an iceberg'

Language Food Appearance

Beliefs
Attitudes
Values
Perceptions

Think about when you do business with someone from another culture. Which visible parts of your culture are most different from theirs? Which invisible parts of your business culture will they find most confusing, or difficult to accept?

The Pyramid model

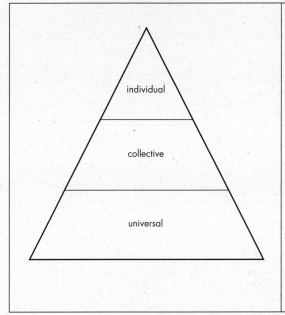

individual

collective

universal

This model of culture was created by Geert Hofstede, one of the most important writers on intercultural communication. He says that culture is a kind of 'software of the mind,' or 'human mental programming'.

There is a **universal** foundation of behaviours that all human beings have in common, such as laughing or crying. Upon this foundation, other behaviours, the **collective**, are learned from the groups we are born into – our families, our companies, our business functions, the teams we join. And yet every person is an **individual** with a unique personality.

Which parts of your behaviour do you think are truly your unique personality? Which parts of your thinking and behaviour come from the groups you are, or have been, a member of?

The Onion model

This model shows how all cultures have at their centre some basic assumptions and values. In some business cultures, for example, there may be an assumption that you can train people to be good leaders. In others the assumption might be that leaders are born, not made.

Beliefs and attitudes are built around these basic assumptions and generate behaviours. For example, if we believe that people are basically lazy, we will develop a concept of leadership which is based on telling people what to do. If we believe that people are basically entrepreneurial, we will develop a leadership approach based on creating opportunities for people to grow into.

Around these basic attitudes, systems, institutions and working processes are created, such as management training systems, goals and rewards.

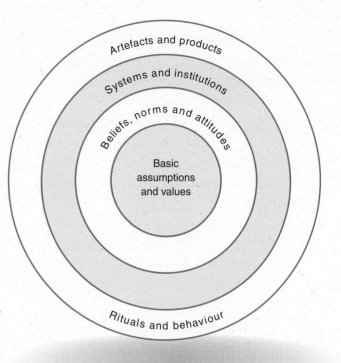

What assumptions about leadership may operate in your culture which may not be shared by people from other cultures?

Preparing for a different culture

If you were travelling abroad to do business in another culture, what would you research so that you could be better prepared? Compare your ideas with the dimensions of culture presented in the next unit.

HOT TIPS

- Remember that other people's behaviours (the *visible*) may be the result of things which you can't see (the *invisible*) and which you don't yet understand
- Understand which parts of your own behaviour are shaped by the different cultural groups you are a part of
- Discuss culture with your international business partners. This way you learn about their culture and they learn about yours

2 Dimensions of national culture – 1

Monochronic or polychronic?

The American anthropologist Edward T Hall was one of the first people to find a systematic way of comparing cultures. He found that most cultures differ from one another in the way they deal with **time** and **information**. In fact, in most cultures the way time is used to organise everyday life and the way information is communicated during tasks are closely related.

Monochronic is the word Hall uses to describe cultures in which the jobs of everyday life are divided up into separate tasks and worked through one at a time. In these cultures the task and the result often has priority over relationships between people. Punctuality and the meeting of deadlines are very important.

Polychronic describes those cultures which do not complete tasks one at a time, but rather do many things at the same time. Relationships between people are more important than the tasks themselves. Keeping people happy and maintaining harmonious relationships can be more important than meeting deadlines. The following story illustrates this difference.

At a multinational company with its HQ in Switzerland, an important meeting of managers is scheduled for 2 p.m. As one of these managers, an American, is approaching the meeting room, he is stopped by one of his staff.

'Excuse me, boss, but I'm having some trouble with this report. Could you help me?'

'Well, I'm on my way to a meeting right now. I'll stop by your office at 4.30 and we'll talk about it then.'

A Brazilian manager is also on his way to the meeting. One of his staff stops him, too, with a request.

'What's the problem?' asks the Brazilian manager, and the two of them discuss the problem for 10 minutes, until it is solved.

The polychronic Brazilian arrives at the meeting five minutes late, but isn't worried by this. The monochronic American, however, is irritated by his colleague's lateness.

Many European, Australian and North American cultures tend to be more monochronic, while many Asian, South American and African cultures tend to be polychronic. However, as we know, culture is complex, and within every individual country you will find differences in monochronic and polychronic behaviour. In Europe, for example, Belgium is divided into monochronic, Dutch-speaking Flanders and polychronic, French-speaking Wallonia.

Professional culture may be a more important factor than national culture. Accountants in monochronic and polychronic cultures may have a similar attitude to time and information, because of the type of work they do.

Which is my approach?

For each pair of statements, tick the one which best describes you. At the end you will see if you have a more monochronic or more polychronic approach.

Monochronic	Polychronic
1 I like to focus on doing one thing at a time.	I often do many things at the same time.
2 I concentrate on finishing a task.	I am happy to be interrupted during tasks.
3 I think deadlines / schedules are very important.	I see deadlines / schedules as things which can be easily changed.
4 I like to arrive on time for meeting.	I tolerate arriving late for meetings.
5 I prioritise time and completing tasks.	I prioritise people and relationships.

Interculturally-effective professionals will understand both their own expectations about time and tasks and the attitudes of their business partners.

Developing flexibility

Use the table to profile people at work who are important for you – managers, colleagues, customers, suppliers. What is their attitude to time? If it is different from your own, think about how you can be flexible and adapt to best work with them. Here are some ideas to help you.

If they are more monochronic than me ...

I need to make sure I arrive at meetings on time.
I should not change deadlines once they have been agreed.

Your own ideas: ....

If they are more polychronic than me ...

I need to spend more time building relationships rather than completing tasks.
I shouldn't focus on deadlines too much as this may irritate others.

Your own ideas: ....

HOT TIPS

- Remember that the way people think about time and the priority they give to tasks and relationships can differ radically across cultures
- Understand your own preferences across these dimensions, and the preferences of your international business partners
- Be flexible and use behaviours which are acceptable to your business partner rather than just expect others to conform to your cultural expectations

3 Dimensions of national culture – 2

Geert Hofstede identified five main dimensions of national culture.

1 Individualism

In **individualistic** cultures people are expected to look after themselves or those very close to them such as family members. Independence and individual responsibility have a strong value. On the contrary, in **collectivist** cultures people see themselves more strongly in terms of a group identity. Loyalty to the group has a higher value than independence and autonomy.

2 Power distance

Power distance is a dimension which describes the hierarchical relationships between individuals in a culture. A **high power distance** culture will have leaders who hold a lot of power and status, who can take decisions without a lot of consultation with those lower in the hierarchy. A **low power distance** culture has less distance between leaders and followers. In a company this could mean that team members will be involved in decision-making and will feel free to disagree with their managers and exchange ideas openly.

3 Uncertainty avoidance

Individuals in **high uncertainty avoidance** cultures do not like risk, and use detailed planning or explicit rules and regulations to manage the unknown and to reduce uncertainty. Cultures with **low uncertainty avoidance** focus less on planning. They value more flexibility, and adaptation to changing circumstances. In business these different attitudes to planning and structure can create significant problems in international teamwork.

4 Masculinity

In more **masculine** cultures gender roles are clearly defined: men are supposed to be assertive, tough, and focused on material success with women more modest, caring, and concerned with the quality of life. In more **feminine** cultures both men and women have a more modest and caring approach, with competitive behaviour valued less.

5 Long-term orientation

Long-term orientation cultures (typical of cultures that have been highly influenced by Confucian philosophy) put great value on long-term planning, traditions, investment and determination to survive in difficult situations. **Short-term orientation** business cultures focus less on tradition and established structures but more on ad hoc organisation in order to achieve quick successes.

Cultural profiling

As we saw with monochronic/polychronic behaviour, these dimensions of culture can help us to describe individuals too. Look at the statements below and answer the questions. You can check your answers on page 153.

1 Individualism

Which of these statements might be made by people with an individualist orientation?

a Before making a decision, I prefer to make sure everyone agrees with it.

b When people do a good job, I think it's good to give them positive personal feedback at team meetings.

c I would not expect to be promoted before someone who was older and who had more experience, even if I could do the job better.

d I focus on achieving my own goals when working in an international team.

2 Power distance

Which of these statements might be made by people with a high power distance orientation?

a I think senior management should eat in the staff canteen at the same tables as everyone else.

b I like my manager because he just gives me a framework and then trusts me to get on with the job independently.

c I don't want team members to openly question my decisions as team manager in meetings.

d It's not my job as a team member to coach other team members. That's the role of the team leader.

3 Uncertainty avoidance

Which of these statements might be made by people with a high uncertainty avoidance orientation?

a I'm not sure that detailed planning is really useful when working in international projects.

b I don't like taking quick decisions without all the facts.

c For an effective meeting, it's vital to have a clear agenda.

d Too much planning limits creativity; we can deal with problems as they arise.

4 Masculinity

Which of these statements might be made by people with a strong masculine orientation?

a I work a seventy-hour week. I always work weekends.

b I don't think managers are paid to be sensitive. They're paid to take tough decisions.

c I see a presentation as a time to do a bit of personal marketing – to get noticed.

d Leadership is all about coaching. It's not simply about telling people what to do.

5 Long-term orientation

Which of these statements might be made by people with a long-term orientation?

a We've always done it this way and I see no reason to change.

b It's OK to spend five years on product development if you know you have a winning product.

c When our company makes a large profit, I think it's best to reinvest in our infrastructure.

d We have to abandon the past if we want to become more innovative.

What does all this mean for daily working life?

Now read all the items again and decide:

* Which are more consistent with the way you think and behave at work?

* Which are consistent with the views and actions of your managers, colleagues and customers?

* What could you do to manage any differences between yourself and others?

HOT TIPS

* Use Hofstede's dimensions as a general orientation to your own national culture and those of your international business partners
* Map your own personal priorities at work across these five dimensions
* Identify possible sources of conflict between your preferences and the preferences of people you work with. Try to be flexible in order to minimise the potential for conflict

4 Culture and values

When we first meet people from other countries or continents, we often notice how they are different from people in our own culture, for example they dress more formally, they smile less, and so on. But at a deeper, universal level, all cultures and people are similar. Because we are all human beings, we all have the same basic problems to solve.

Florence Rockwood Kluckhohn identified five problems common to all human groups, which she called **value orientations**. These can be read as a series of questions with a limited range of answers.

1 Human nature orientation

What is the fundamental character of human nature? Are people by nature basically evil, basically good, or are they a mixture of good and evil? In business, this may have an effect on how leaders manage their staff. Those who think people are basically lazy may monitor and control more than those who believe that people are self-motivated.

2 Person vs. nature orientation

What kind of relationship should human beings have with nature? Should people submit to the power of nature, try to live in harmony with nature, or try to control nature? This will have an effect on attitudes to planning and structuring working life. For example, modern capitalism is strongly founded on the belief that the environment can be controlled for man's benefit. In developing countries with poor infrastructure, this sense of control is not as strong.

3 Time orientation

How do people think about time? For example, when solving a problem, do we look for the answer in past traditions and standards, in the present situation, or is our focus forward-looking and in future possibilities? This may be seen in business in attitudes to planning and risk – do we analyse the past to make sure things don't go wrong in the future, or do we move directly into the future with a 'can do' mentality?

4 Activity orientation

What is the meaning of life? Why are we here? Is our purpose to *do* things, in which case working and being busy has a moral value? Or does life have a more spiritual purpose, for example we move to a higher level when we die? Or is life simply focused in the here and now?

5 Relational orientation

How should status be given to ourselves and others? How should a person answer the question *Who am I?* For example do I answer this question by explaining my family and relationships as in some cultures, or do I answer by explaining what groups I belong to – my clan, my profession, the football team I support? Or do I describe myself primarily as an individual and the things that I have achieved alone?

The fact that communities of people answer these questions in more or less the same way identifies them as a culture. And the answers that one set of people give can be compared with those of another group, giving us points of difference in the fundamental values of the two cultures.

Your own culture's value system

Think about your own national culture for a moment. On the lines below put a mark along the scale to show how your culture answers these universal questions. It is possible to make more than one mark. For example, if you think your culture puts equal emphasis on the past *and* the future, you should mark them both.

When answering the questions, don't mark down your own opinions (which would correspond to the individual peak in Hofstede's pyramid in Unit 1), but rather try to put down the opinions of most of the people who come from the same village or city that you come from. This will give *collective* answers to the questions. If possible, discuss with other members of your own culture to see if you agree on the fundamental values of the culture.

1 Deep down, people are really ...

evil	a mixture of good and evil	good

2 As regards human beings' relationship to nature, I think ...

nature is in control	there is harmony with nature	we have mastery over nature

3 When solving important problems, it's most important to consider ...

the past	the present	the future

4 We were put on this earth to ...

be (relax and enjoy)	become something higher (spiritual purpose)	do things (complete tasks and get results)

5 I explain who I am by describing ...

my ancestors in the past	the groups I belong to	myself alone

Now compare your own cultures with other cultures in the world, starting with those you do business with and have experience of.

Try to identify cultures which are different in their value orientations in some way. What kinds of cultural misunderstandings might result from differences in these value orientations? How could you try to deal with these misunderstandings?

HOT TIPS

Remember:
- As human beings we all face the same basic challenges
- We solve these challenges in different ways based on different cultural values
- Finding what we have in common is as important as identifying what is different

5 Understanding corporate culture

Many of the concepts in Units 1, 2 and 3 have been applied to business organisations by John Mole, a consultant in cross-cultural management, in his book *Mind Your Manners: Managing Business Cultures in Europe*. He focuses particularly on two aspects of corporate culture: organisation and leadership.

Organisation

Organisation is a way to plan human activity. There are different attitudes to organisation. At one end of the spectrum is **systematic** organisation, where planning and task completion in a defined sequence (monochronic) is prioritised. At the other end of the spectrum is **organic** organisation, which is characterised by the idea of a business as a social organisation, made up of human beings. Like polychronic cultures, organic organisations are more people-centred.

Leadership

This dimension is similar to Hofstede's idea of individualism versus collectivism (see Unit 3). At one end of the leadership spectrum is the belief that leadership should be carried out by the best and most capable **individuals**, and that these leaders should have power over their followers (high power distance).

At the **group** end of the spectrum there is the belief that everyone in the organisation has a right to give their opinions. Leaders are allowed to lead as long as they follow the wishes of the majority of the people they represent. This ideal of democratic leadership corresponds to collectivism and low power distance.

Which form of organisation and leadership do you prefer?

The Mole Map

John Mole sets up these two dimensions to make a grid which has become known as the Mole Map. This can be used to locate any organisation along the Company Structure and Leadership Style axes.

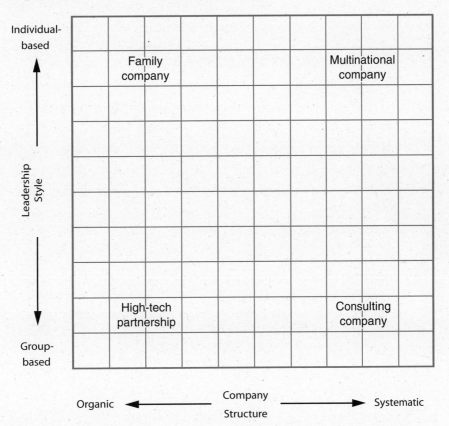

The Mole Map also helps us to identify four typical corporate cultures.

The first are those companies which combine organic organisation with individual leadership. The typical organisation here is the family company, with a leading patriarch or matriarch, a strong set of traditions and a strong (family) network of relationships.

Second are companies which have systematic organisation and individual leadership. Their archetype is the multinational company, typically led by someone who has worked their way up through the world of business to arrive in a position of centralised authority. These companies often have formal systems of training which make such promotion possible.

The third kind have a combination of systematic organisation with group leadership. These companies are often run by well-organised specialists who have well-defined targets. The archetype of this kind of company is a large accounting or consulting agency.

Finally, there are those companies which have organic organisation and group leadership. Both decision-making and profits are equally shared. Organisation is flexible, changing to fit external situations and internal relationships between members. The archetype is the creative, high-tech partnership.

Profiling culture using the Mole Map

Use the Mole Map to analyse different cultures in which you work.

– What is the culture of your company, the function in which you work (HR, finance or marketing) and your specific department?

– Which type of culture is the easiest for you to work in, and which is the most difficult?

– How well do you adapt to working in a culture which has different values from your own?

– What could you do to adapt better?

HOT TIPS

- You need to understand the different organisational and functional cultures which are part of your working life
- You should understand in which cultures you feel more comfortable
- You need to be flexible enough to work within cultures whose values and explicit behaviours may not match exactly your own

Understanding yourself

'Culture hides more than it reveals and, strangely enough, what it hides, it hides most effectively from its own participants. Years of study have convinced me that the real job is not to understand foreign culture but to understand our own.' Edward T Hall

The way small children learn their first language is fascinating: they seem to learn so naturally and with such ease. And it's not just their native language that they learn. Children also learn when to shout and when to whisper, how and when to make eye contact, how close to stand to different people, and when it is their turn to speak. In fact, all of us learn a complete code of behaviours as we grow up in our home society. We come to know what is right in specific circumstances and what is not.

This code of behaviour is perhaps the most important aspect of our culture. And because most people around us follow the same code, it seems easy and natural. We are in our element, like a fish in water, and our way of doing things becomes the only way. Like our native language, our own culture becomes second nature. It is so effortless, that it becomes **invisible**.

But in order to understand how people from other cultures react to us, and what sort of impression we give them, we must spend time learning about ourselves. We need to understand our own ways of thinking and seeing things. We must make our natural way of doing things **visible** to ourselves so we can become open to the ways that others do things.

In this module we will move away from models of national and corporate culture to look at personal identity and ways of thinking and feeling.

The next five units will help you to understand yourself, and give you ideas and techniques on how to manage yourself more effectively across cultures.

6 Culture and the individual

7 Opinions and cultural values

8 The emotional component of culture

9 Dealing with ambiguity

10 The D-I-E model

6 Culture and the individual

As we saw in Module 1, there are many ways to understand and describe culture. There are detailed scientific descriptions of cultural dimensions based on empirical data. There are models looking like icebergs or pyramids or onions. There are simple explanations of 'the way we do things around here.'

Think again of Hofstede's pyramid model in Unit 1: at the universal level all people are alike, simply because we are all human beings. Then we are deeply influenced by the groups we belong to, the collective level of culture. The collective level of culture is complex because we are members of so many groups – nation, region, company, team, family, and so on. And finally we are all unique individuals as well.

Here is a second onion model which allows us to understand ourselves and how we think and operate in business. It shows our identity made of many layers of different group cultures with personality at the centre.

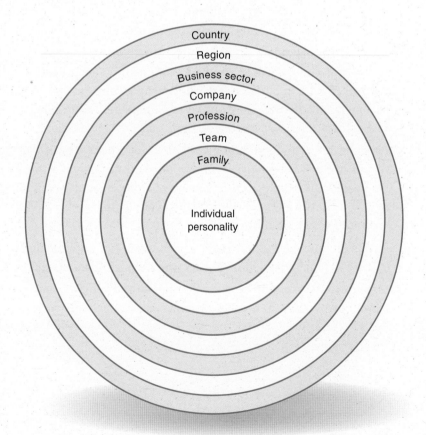

Understanding who we are

Look at the example *International Profile* below which uses the second onion model to understand an individual – his or her range of values, behaviours and attitudes – from their culture background.

INTERNATIONAL PROFILE: PATRICK BAYBEAUD

Cultural profile

Patrick is a senior manager in a French pharmaceuticals company. He is French and was born on the French island of Martinique in the Caribbean, and studied in Paris before settling there after his studies.

He trained as a chemist and then joined a large multinational American pharmaceuticals company, working for a number of years in research and development based in the US. He is now based back in Paris and heads a project team whose task is to standardise IT solutions across the European business units.

Professional profile

Patrick is a successful international manager. His Martinique background developed in him social skills and a strong sense of the importance of relationships which has been important later in his management career during difficult change processes.

His scientific studies taught him the value of collecting and analysing data before taking decisions, although this has proved a problem in recent projects with marketing colleagues who often have a desire to move more quickly to a decision in order to satisfy customer requests.

His time in the United States taught him the value of participatory management, of involving people in decision-making. However, this was problematic when he first returned to take up a management position in Paris, where the leadership culture was more top down. Nevertheless, he has learned to fit in and has now developed a more directive leadership style which works in the Paris environment.

Finally, his natural sense of humour, which he has had ever since he was a young child and was supported in his family environment, has enabled him to remain positive during recent project work which has involved painful change for many local business units, creating resistance and conflict at many international meetings.

Who are you?

Write a short International Profile for yourself which describes your background and how it has shaped and shapes the way you think and act at work, for example, being punctual; working in hierarchies; not taking risks; the way you make decisions – logically or intuitively; whether you put tasks or people at the centre of work; and your ideas of good leadership. Look back at Module 1 for more ideas.

INTERNATIONAL PROFILE

Cultural profile
Professional profile

Self-knowledge is a core competence for interculturally-effective people. It is essential to have an understanding of your own culture and how it has shaped how you think, feel and react to other people and difficult-to-understand situations.

This knowledge will help you to understand and use your own personal strengths. It will also help you to adapt your work or communication style to deal with people from other cultural backgrounds.

HOT TIPS

- Use the onion model in this unit to understand yourself and others
- Become aware of your own strengths and weaknesses by profiling yourself
- Decide on steps to maximise your strengths and minimise your weaknesses

7 Opinions and cultural values

In this unit we explore the role that culture plays in forming opinions and value judgements. If you can understand how culture affects the way you think and why other people might think differently from you, then you can become more open to other points of view.

Look at the general opinions expressed in the boxes below. Mark each box with a tick if you agree with the opinion, or with a cross if you disagree.

A person is always innocent until proven guilty.	Life is a spiritual journey: you should reach a higher level before you die.	The present moment is all we have. Eat, drink and be merry, for tomorrow we die.
Human beings should always be very careful not to pollute their environment.	Some people are born to lead; others are born to follow.	Be careful when talking to strangers: they can be either good or bad.
A person is important because of who they are, not because of what they do.	We should learn from history; in the past things were simpler and better.	People are powerless when confronted with God or Fate. What will be will be.
The best form of decision-making is group consensus.	You have to look out for yourself; otherwise people will take advantage of you.	A person's value is measured by their achievements.
Careful planning makes great things possible: a little sacrifice today will bring a better tomorrow.	Humans are nature's greatest creation, and they have a right to control and perfect nature.	A free society allows its individuals to express disagreement.

Opinions express our values

The opinions on the previous page all express a value orientation. Look back at the five value orientations you read about in Unit 4: each one is represented by one of the five box colours (white, dark grey, light grey, dark orange, light orange). See if you can match them up. You can check your answers on page 153.

1 Human nature: _____

2 Person vs. Nature: _____

3 Time: _____

4 Activity: _____

5 Relational: _____

Now look at the colour of the boxes you have ticked and you will see how your opinions connect to certain value areas. Which are most important for you? How does your general working style and the way you communicate, for example in meetings and by email, reflect these value areas? Look at the self-analysis below and write a similar example for yourself.

> 'I ticked white a lot. And I think my working style reflects the value of doing rather than thinking. I am very results-oriented and I like to work to high quality standards at work. In meetings I can be pretty direct and, sometimes, a little impatient. I suppose I am quite ambitious. Outside of work, though, I am a very different person.'

Finding a way to live, work and communicate with each other

In an international business setting we exchange opinions all the time in meetings and informal discussions. These opinions often express core values. Interculturally-effective people are able to express their opinions in ways which are not only clear to people from other cultures, but which also show respect for their values.

🌐 TRACK 2   Listen to a short extract from a business meeting where the participants Caroline, Angela and Bob are discussing a software problem. In your opinion, which person does not communicate sensitively? Why not? You can read the audioscript and compare some possible answers on page 153.

Negotiating opinions

Intercultural communication, like negotiation, only works if you are able to compromise. In doing business with people from other cultures you will meet values, attitudes and opinions that you strongly disagree with. You don't have to give up your own values, of course, but you should think about expressing them in a way that is diplomatic and not confrontational. One way to do this is to synthesise the different opinions into a compromise opinion which both parties can agree with.

From the previous page, choose two pairs of boxes of the same colour where you marked one with a tick and the other with a cross. Try to write a compromise opinion that expresses the core values of both boxes. For example:

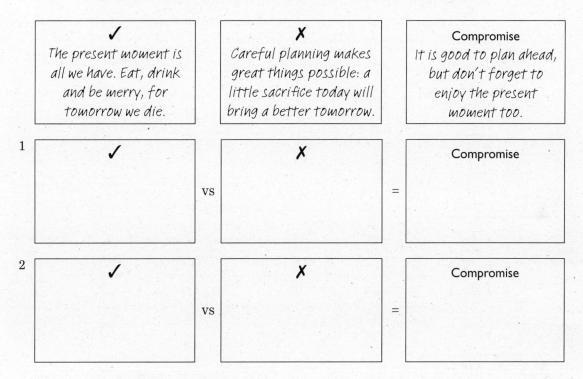

To be culturally effective, you need to communicate respectfully with those people whose values are not the same as your own.

– Which people at work have very different attitudes and opinions from yours?

– How effectively do you think you exchange opinions with them?

– How useful would it be to focus more on finding compromises?

HOT TIPS

- Be open to those with different values from your own
- Express your opinions in a way which respects the opinions of others
- Find common ground between your opinions and those of others. This can be an effective way to build mutual respect and common understanding

8 The emotional component of culture

An intercultural meeting

An American businessman who had been very successful in negotiating important sales agreements in one part of the world was sent to another part of the world to do a similar job. He returned to headquarters without a signed agreement. Here is an extract from his report.

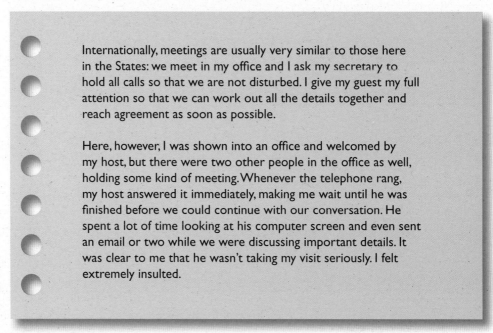

> Internationally, meetings are usually very similar to those here in the States: we meet in my office and I ask my secretary to hold all calls so that we are not disturbed. I give my guest my full attention so that we can work out all the details together and reach agreement as soon as possible.
>
> Here, however, I was shown into an office and welcomed by my host, but there were two other people in the office as well, holding some kind of meeting. Whenever the telephone rang, my host answered it immediately, making me wait until he was finished before we could continue with our conversation. He spent a lot of time looking at his computer screen and even sent an email or two while we were discussing important details. It was clear to me that he wasn't taking my visit seriously. I felt extremely insulted.

What do you think happened here? On one level it's relatively easy to understand. In Unit 2 we looked at the difference between monochronic and polychronic cultures, a difference which is clearly at work here.

However, the root of the problem is not just understanding what the differences are, but also the emotional reaction that we have to behaviour which differs from our own. The American 'felt extremely insulted' that his host didn't give him all his attention, although his host certainly didn't intend to insult him.

This is what we call a **critical incident**: a conflict that arises between people from different cultures when both of them do the right thing according to his or her own culture, but which the other culture finds unacceptable.

When we communicate with people from our own culture, we have realistic expectations about how they will react and we can quite accurately predict and interpret their behaviour.

When interacting with people who have been socialised differently from ourselves, our predictions of their behaviour become less accurate. And when their behaviour doesn't meet our expectations, we are likely to react emotionally. As Richard Brislin explains:

> 'An instinctive human response to such a challenge is to categorize people into two classes: *us* and *them*. *We* and *ours* become the centre of what is reasonable and normal in life. *They* and *theirs* represent the strange and the potentially dangerous.'

This is called **ethnocentrism**, and together with ambiguity, which we'll be looking at in Unit 9, is one of the major problems which people face when communicating across cultures. We give a certain meaning to ways of behaving, and we are surprised, insulted or threatened when other people give those same behaviours a different meaning. These different interpretations are at the centre of most intercultural misunderstandings.

The most effective way to combat misinterpretation and ethnocentrism is to become conscious of our cultural expectations, and to modify them if necessary. This is what we will examine over the next three units.

How to deal with ethnocentrism and emotions

In his book *The Art of Crossing Cultures*, the American interculturalist Craig Storti describes the dynamic process of experiencing people different from ourselves. He offers the following flow chart to help us better understand the process:

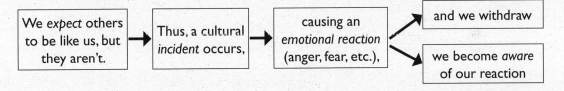

After the emotional reaction, it's difficult to stay calm and to remain in control of our own reactions. Most people withdraw in some way from the situation. But if they do this every time, no intercultural learning takes place.

If, however, we go into an intercultural situation knowing that we may have the wrong expectations, and knowing that we may react emotionally to the situation, we can be more aware of our own thoughts and behaviour and try to control ourselves and learn from the experience. Here is Storti's diagram of this next part of the experience:

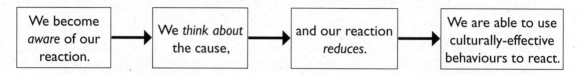

The ability to control our emotions when working with people who are different from ourselves is a key intercultural competence. It's important not to make negative judgements too quickly, but to remain open to other ways of thinking. As emotions arise, we need to engage, become curious, and learn about the values and attitudes which drive the behaviour of the other person. In this way we can reduce the amount of potentially damaging conflict.

Think about a cultural incident you have experienced in your professional working life. How did people behave which was different from your expectation? How did you feel? What did you do to control your emotions and react positively? What could you have done differently? What will you do if a similar thing happens again?

HOT TIPS

- Try to react rationally, not emotionally, when people do things differently from what you expect
- Work hard to understand people who challenge you emotionally. In this way, you can get ideas from those with very different points of view

9 Dealing with ambiguity

When dealing with people from foreign cultures, international business people are often in a situation where they must make decisions without having all the necessary information. This is called **ambiguity**, and goes hand-in-hand with ethnocentrism as a major obstacle to cross-cultural understanding.

Tolerance for ambiguity is one of the keys to success in intercultural interactions. The more tolerance we have for ambiguous situations, the more comfortable we will feel in situations where we don't have all the information we need. Research shows that people who aren't worried by ambiguity are more successful in working in foreign environments.

One way to train for ambiguous situations is to adopt a 'wait and see' attitude towards behaviours that are strange or that don't immediately make sense to us. We need to think about what is going on behind the behaviour in order to clarify and adjust, or **reframe**, our understanding of the situation.

The next exercise gives you practice in reframing ambiguous situations. Read the descriptions of four different behaviours and then write down your interpretation of each one – that is, what the behaviour means in your own culture.

1 A civil servant refuses to perform a necessary service for you until you pay him an extra amount of money above the set fee.

   Your interpretation: ....

   ....

2 A colleague arrives at 14.30 for a meeting which started at 14.00.

   Your interpretation: ....

   ....

3 The young person you are interviewing avoids eye contact throughout the interview.

   Your interpretation: ....

   ....

4 A person normally takes over two hours for his lunch break.

   Your interpretation: ....

   ....

Now read these explanations of the people's behaviour.

1 In this culture civil servants are paid so little that they can only survive by taking such payments.

2 In this culture meetings never start until at least 30 minutes past the stated starting time.

3 In this culture it is a sign of disrespect to make eye contact with anyone older than yourself.

4 In this culture people normally work until 7 or 8 p.m.

With this new information, how would you reframe your interpretations of the people's behaviour?

As you can see, once you have additional information, it's easy to reframe a certain type of behaviour and give it a different interpretation. This is the key to successful intercultural communication: don't make a judgement immediately and, if possible, manage your emotional reactions until you have all the information you need to fully understand a situation.

HOT TIPS

- Slow down your judgement process and accept that you need more information before you can interpret what you see
- Become more patient when working across cultures – collecting more information will take more time than you are used to spending
- Think about how you think

10 The D-I-E model

Building on the ideas of Unit 9, in this unit we show you a model of perception which will help you think more openly about unfamiliar situations.

As we've already seen in this module, effective international communicators need to think a lot about *how* they think. If we become more aware of how our values and assumptions affect our thinking, how we interpret what is around us, we can become more open to other points of view.

Let's start with a short exercise. Take a close look at the picture opposite and *describe* what you see. Write your ideas in fewer than 100 words.

....
....
....
....
....
....
....

Typically, people write down 'descriptions' like these:

> *The kids are a little nervous.*
> *He's a dancer showing his kids some dance moves.*
> *It's a father playing with his children.*
> *It's a fun picture.*

The interesting thing about these example 'descriptions' is that they aren't descriptions at all. They are **interpretations** of the picture – assumptions about what is happening. In fact, the final sentence is an **evaluation** – an emotional judgement about whether it's a nice picture or not.

True neutral descriptions of the picture would be more like this:

There's a boy and a girl.   *There are two children.*
The boy's wearing an anorak.   *A man is in the air.*
The girl has a fringe.   *There are trees in the background.*

Now look at your own 'descriptions' – how many are truly describing the picture, how many are interpreting it and how many are evaluating it?

The D-I-E model of perception and thinking

When we interact with the world around us, our thinking has three important phases:

D Describe First we collect information by seeing or hearing what is happening.

I Interpret Then we make a judgement about the meaning of what we can see or hear.

E Evaluate Finally, we feel something or have an emotional reaction, for example we like or don't like it.

The problem with human beings is that we usually interpret and evaluate the actions and words of others too quickly.

This works well enough when we interact with people from the same culture. We can move to interpretation more quickly because there are shared ways of seeing and common understanding. We know what a greeting means, or the purpose of a handshake, or a bow, or an invitation to dinner. However, when working in a foreign culture it isn't always easy to know exactly what is going on around us. Because we are outsiders, we don't always have all the information necessary to interpret the situations we are in accurately. We need to slow down and be careful not to make interpretations too quickly based on our own cultural and personal values.

Slowing down with the D-I-E model

When we're working across cultures it's important to be able to slow down and control our perception, and take the time to collect as much information as possible about what we see. Only in this way can we make an effective assessment of what other people are doing and saying to us, so that we can take the right decisions about what we do and communicate.

The D-I-E process of thinking (first **describe**, then **interpret** and finally **evaluate**) gives us a model to slow down and control our perception. If we practise thinking using the D-I-E process, we can stop ourselves from jumping to conclusions too quickly. We make ourselves really look at what is happening and question if what we are seeing is just our interpretation.

Use D-I-E to describe the picture below.

1   Describe what you see. Be neutral and exact, giving details of what you actually see in the picture. It's just the facts, not your opinion.

2   Now interpret what you see. Your interpretation includes both your opinion of the meaning of the picture and what motives the people in the picture may have for behaving the way that they do.

3   Finally, evaluate the picture. Your evaluation is an emotional judgement about what you see. Is the situation good or bad, right or wrong? What do you feel about it? Do you like the picture, or not?

Compare your answers with the example on page 153.

....
....
....
....
....
....
....
....

Applying D-I-E to everyday business life

D-I-E isn't simply a process for describing pictures. It's also a methodology for interacting with people from different cultures in your everyday business life.

Tips for describing

Spend time observing and describing what people are doing – spend time listening to the actual words they're saying. Work hard to stop yourself interpreting and just focus on collecting data.

Tips for interpreting

Hear yourself making those first interpretations which are probably based on your own cultural and personal values and preferences. Try to generate *alternative* interpretations (similar to the reframing you did in Unit 9) based on sensitivity to the other person's culture and personality.

Tips for evaluating

Hear yourself switching off your first evaluation (*I don't like that idea.*). Perhaps decide not to evaluate at all, but simply to ask questions to learn more about the motivation of the other person. Or just respect their way of doing things as different from your own and find a way to work with them.

🔊 TRACK 3   Listen to a British businessman describing, interpreting and evaluating a presentation he gave abroad. What will he do next time, and how does he think he will feel? You can read the audio script and check your answers on page 153.

HOT TIPS

- Take time to collect information with careful observation and description
- Don't trust your first interpretation of events – practise imagining how others might see events
- Try to control negative emotions that you feel which are caused by your own cultural values

Listening effectively

'Three quarters of the miseries and misunderstandings in the world would finish if people were to put on the shoes of their adversaries and understood their points of view.' Mahatma Gandhi

Many professionals underestimate the potential for miscommunication across cultures. They say, 'There is one international business culture now.' or 'IT people understand each other across the world.' Although there is some truth here, it is also true that miscommunication is still a major cause of inefficiency in the international workplace.

In Module 2 we saw how interpretation can generate misunderstanding and conflict. In the next two modules we look at the challenges which individuals face as they try to build common understanding. We introduce a number of ideas for listening (Module 3) and speaking (Module 4) which support clear and effective communication.

In this module the focus is on listening behaviours. We start by investigating potential sources of miscommunication in business conversations caused by different values and different styles.

11 Understanding miscommunication across cultures

12 The purpose of listening

13 Listening – attitude and style

14 The E-N-G-A-G-E-M-E-N-T approach

15 Using questions to listen

11 Understanding miscommunication across cultures

Communicating *seems* to be a relatively easy thing to do. You just open your mouth and speak, or you just relax and listen to the words of other people. However, communication is actually an extremely complex process which experts still have problems in understanding.

In Unit 4 we described the 'iceberg' model of culture: the objects and behaviours in the small area above the surface, with values and beliefs in the huge area below the water line. In many ways communication is also an iceberg. I can hear what you say, and I can see what you write. But what I can't see is the area below the surface – inside your head – to know what you are thinking, why you said what you said, what is the true motivation or intention behind your message. I have to *interpret* to understand what you really meant.

In Unit 9 we looked at how quickly people interpret pictures from their own point of view. The same process goes on during every conversation and discussion. People don't just hear the words others speak. They have to interpret them through subjective filters – cultural and psychological. And in doing so, they create new and unintended meanings, and so misunderstanding begins.

Miscommunication is the one certainty in communication

In his book *The Art of Crossing Cultures* Craig Storti documented several examples of miscommunication in his observation of Greek-American conversations during a period of work in Greece. He uses actual dialogues to show how different values and attitudes surface in conversation and can cause miscommunication.

Try out your own intercultural sensitivity. Read the first part of one of Storti's short dialogues between an American manager and his Greek team member. Note down what you believe is the thinking of each individual during the conversation – why did they say what they said, how did they interpret the other person? Check your answers on page 154.

Part 1

What they said		What they were thinking	
American	How long will it take you to finish this report?	**American**	....
Greek	I don't know. How long should it take?	**Greek**	....
American	You're in the best position to analyse time requirements.	**American**	....
Greek	Ten days.	**Greek**	....
American	Take 15. Is it agreed you'll do it in 15 days?	**American**	....

After this initial conversation, the Greek went to work on the report. In fact, it needed 30 days of regular work. So the Greek worked day and night, but at the end of the 15th day, he still needed one more day's work. And so the two met again.

Read Part 2 and make notes, as you did for Part 1. Check your answers on page 154.

Part 2

What they said		What they were thinking	
American	Where is my report?	**American**	....
Greek	It will be ready tomorrow.	**Greek**	....
American	But we had agreed that it would be ready today.	**American**	....
Greek	This is unacceptable. I resign.	**Greek**	....

The American is speechless and surprised!

The risk of monologues rather than dialogue

In these two very short conversations, we can see how cultural and personal differences in expectations of leadership, team role, decision-making process, time, and business relationships can produce serious miscommunication. Although the two people talked to each other, it was more like two monologues than a true dialogue. Both thought there was some form of common understanding, but in reality there was none. Neither communicator used special listening techniques, for example asking clarifying questions, or speaking techniques such as checking understanding, to get their message across clearly. There was no cultural intelligence during the communication – there was just poor communication.

Unfortunately, this is the reality of a great deal of intercultural and interpersonal communication.

Which listening and speaking techniques do you think make conversations more effective? Note your ideas below.

Effective listening techniques	Effective speaking techniques
1 *Don't assume that you understand. Ask questions to clarify.*	1 *Don't assume that other people have understood you. Ask them if they understood or agree with what you just said.*

As you go through the rest of the units in this module and the next, compare your ideas with the ones you read about.

HOT TIPS

- Remember, you are like an iceberg when communicating: people can hear what you say, but not why you are saying it
- Anticipate misunderstanding. Ask questions to clarify what others say
- Develop your listening and speaking skills with the techniques explained in the next units

12 The purpose of listening

Why do we listen to other people? Think about this for a few minutes. Can you think of ten different reasons why you listen to people? It may seem a strange question. But unless we understand the scope and value of listening as a human activity, it's unlikely that we can ever become effective listeners.

Ten reasons for listening to other people

1 **To acquire relevant and accurate information**
Notice that this is a reason for listening motivated by self-interest – I listen because I need information. When we listen for self-interest, we often close our ears to other important messages from the speaker. We miss things.

2 **To assess the competence and trustworthiness of the other person**
This is an important reason for listening in business. Listening here focuses on analysing the expertise of the speaker from their comments on business issues, and judging their attitudes to business relationships and ethics.

3 **To show competence and build trust**
Commenting intelligently on what the other person is saying allows others to understand our expertise.

   🎧 TRACK 4   Listen to a short discussion during a meeting in which Per-Erik, a consultant, listens very carefully to a potential customer, Alan. Which of Per-Erik's comments convinces Alan that he is the right business partner? You can read the audio script and check your answers on page 154.

4 **To show respect and build rapport**
Listening is an important way to give time to others and show commitment to the relationship. Remember, those from task-oriented cultures may expect quiet behaviour from their listeners, but those from more relationship-driven contexts expect a more active listener who participates with plenty of comments and positive feedback.

5 **To gain control by understanding how to influence**
Effective influencers and motivators try to understand the other person's interests before speaking. Typical behaviours here are clarifying and summarising to ensure correct understanding before trying to persuade.

6 **To empathise and make others feel good**
Good listeners are sometimes just there for other people when they want to talk about a problem or a difficult situation. Listening in this context means making the speaker feel that he or she is understood sympathetically.

🔊 **TRACK 5**   Listen to two short conversations. Which listener do you think is more effective, and why? You can read the audio script and check your answers on pages 154–5.

7   **To note the communication style of the speaker and then adapt one's own style to it, to make communication comfortable for the other person**
Listening here is focused on recognising and adapting flexibly to the communication style of the other person in terms of verbal and non-verbal behaviour. The listener adapts their own behaviour to that of the speaker to create a smooth communication interface.

8   **To analyse the mindset of the other person**
Listening can also be used to assess the psychology or mindset of a speaker. This can be important when working with people whose cultural values are very different.

🔊 **TRACK 6**   Listen to a short extract from a presentation. A listener in the audience asks a question to clarify the presenter's attitude towards time and quality in his project. What answer does he get? You can read the audio script and check your answers on page 155.

9   **To hear how far our own ideas have been understood and valued**
We all need to feel we are being listened to, that our thoughts are valued and respected. If we don't hear our own ideas and concerns reflected back as important, we may begin to feel anxious and make a negative judgement about the person we're talking with – 'Hey, why don't you listen to me for a change?'

10   **To give pleasure**
People should enjoy talking to you. Do people say of you that you're an easy person to talk to, that it's fun to have a conversation or meeting with you? If people are motivated to talk to you, it's likely you'll get the best from them.

HOT TIPS

- Don't assume that you're a good listener. You'll be closer to the truth if you assume that you're a *bad* listener
- Balance your needs with the needs of the speaker when deciding how to listen
- Listening is an important management tool – make it your priority to become an excellent listener across cultures

13 Listening – attitude and style

Developing a listening style

The biggest barrier to effective listening is usually ourselves. We often listen with the wrong attitude and the wrong style. Effective listeners develop the right attitudes and have a range of listening styles which they can match to different speakers. Let's take a look at these attitudes and styles.

The right attitude to listening

Listening across cultures can be challenging. There's the stress of working in a foreign language, of listening to difficult accents, of trying to understand unfamiliar mindsets. In these circumstances, it's important to develop three positive attitudes to listening.

Attitude 1 The speaker is saying something important

When we feel that a message isn't important for us, we tend to switch off. Many people stop listening and start thinking about what they want to say while the other person is still telling them things. Effective listeners give time to others.

Attitude 2 Respect the speaker's style of speaking

Speakers sometimes make it difficult for listeners to follow them. They speak too quickly or slowly. They give too much or too little information. They speak too loudly or quietly. They speak too emotionally or too neutrally. As listeners, it's important to be tolerant towards speakers with a 'difficult' speaking style.

Attitude 3 Always clarify

As we have seen in earlier units, we often misinterpret what people are saying to us because of our own cultural and psychological filters. Effective listeners never assume that they have understood. They always take time to check they understand what people have said.

🎧 **TRACK 7** Listen to three short dialogues. In which one does the listener show a positive attitude? Why do the listeners in the other two dialogues fail to listen? You can read the audio script and compare your answers on page 155.

The right style for listening internationally

People have different listening styles. Some listen silently, others with questions. Some listen for information, others for emotions. It's important to know your own listening style in order to know how to interact with others effectively.

Read the following descriptions of three fundamental listening styles. Which describes your style?

Style 1   People-focused listeners – relationship cultures

This listening style prioritises the relationship between the speaker and the listener. The listener works very hard to support the speaker by asking the right question or by giving positive feedback. This type of listener has a lot of patience and can really make the speaker feel 'listened' to.

However, people who listen in this way may spend a lot of time asking small talk questions. They may not spend enough time focusing on the hard content of what is said. As a result, this listening style may come across as unfocused, especially to speakers from information and result-oriented cultures. Some speakers may feel the listener is too *nice*, perhaps even superficial, and doesn't spend enough time telling the speaker his or her own opinions.

Style 2   Information-oriented listeners – data cultures

This listening style focuses on collecting and analysing data in order to understand a situation as fully as possible. This type of listener can be patient and will usually take the time to hear all the information. This is very true in meetings because this type of listener wants to take decisions based on all the available evidence.

However, these listeners may overlook the relationship aspect of communication. For some speakers this listening style may be too serious and focus too much on data. The listener may come across as rather cold or unsympathetic to a speaker from a more relationship-oriented culture.

Style 3   Result-oriented listeners – action cultures

These listeners have one primary interest: to get to the goal as quickly and as efficiently as possible. They have little patience for irrelevant information. They can get frustrated by speakers who talk for too long and who give too much information. They like speakers who know what they want and give the necessary information to support an opinion. These listeners may interrupt a lot or try to convince others quickly.

Some speakers will see this listening style as a little pushy and arrogant. Result-oriented listeners are happy to disagree openly and directly if they think it will get them to a result quickly. Some speakers will also see the style as superficial because the result-oriented listener makes decisions before collecting all the necessary information.

TRACK 8 Listen to Jean-Paul in extracts from three different management meetings. Which listening style does he use in each meeting? You can read the audio script and check your answers on pages 155–6.

1 ....

2 ....

3 ....

Effective international listeners adapt their style to the person and the context.

Now create a short *Personal listening profile* by answering the following questions. Note down your ideas in the box below.

a Which listening style is my main style?

b In which ways am I good listener internationally?

c In which ways am I a bad listener internationally?

d How can I improve my listening skills (attitudes and styles) for working across cultures?

> **Personal listening profile**
>
>

HOT TIPS

- Show respect to people by listening carefully to what they tell you. It might not be important for you, but it may be to them
- Never assume that you have fully understood what someone has just said to you
- Know your own listening style and adapt it where necessary to the needs of the situation and the speaker

14 The E-N-G-A-G-E-M-E-N-T approach

The secret to becoming an effective listener across cultures is attitude. Effective listeners truly believe that it is important to give time to listening to other people, particularly to those who express very different opinions and beliefs from their own. If you listen with this positive attitude, you will engage speakers to work openly and positively with you.

Listening is about **engagement**: engaging yourself with others, engaging with diversity and, as a result, engaging others with you. Let's look now at how to listen effectively using the E-N-G-A-G-E-M-E-N-T model.

E **Engagement** starts by emptying your mind of your own thoughts as the other person begins to talk to you. Make a conscious effort to tell yourself to concentrate fully on what's being said.

N **Never** disturb the person talking to you. Listen to yourself listening and, if you hear any of the unconstructive thoughts below, switch them off and re-engage with the speaker and what they are saying.

Unconstructive thought	What you're doing
'I have other things to do.'	focusing on your own agenda
'This is boring.'	rejecting importance
'You're wrong.'	contradicting
'That's enough about this. Let's talk about ...'	changing the subject
'You don't need to worry about that.'	rejecting feelings
'Let me tell what happened to me.'	transferring to yourself
'If I were you, I would ...'	advising

G **Give** positive feedback, both verbally and non-verbally, in ways which the speaker can understand.

A **Allow** others time to say what they want to say – be patient.

G **Give** feedback to yourself on your own listening performance *as* you listen. Ask yourself – am I listening well enough, am I concentrating on the other person, am I asking the right questions, am I getting bored?

E **Eliminate** any negative emotions you may feel towards speakers whom you feel are ignoring, disrespecting or attacking you.

M   **Make** others talk to you by asking questions. Good listeners create opportunities for themselves to listen to their own questions being answered.

E   **Energise** yourself the moment you feel tired or you start to lose interest.

N   **Note-taking** is an excellent way to maintain concentration when listening to a long presentation or a number of inputs from speakers during a meeting.

T   **Try** the **key word** approach to listening. This means mentally noting key words a speaker uses when talking to you. You then use the key words as a basis for developing the conversation to clarify what the speaker meant:

You said that the deadline was now 'a problem'. What do you mean by 'problem' exactly?

or to comment on what was said, or to further expand the discussion:

When you said 'it's important to ask customers what they need', I totally agree. In our business division we do formal surveys twice a year to collect customer feedback ...

🎧 **TRACK 9**   Listen to a conversation in which Roberto uses the key word approach in order to clarify what Ian is saying. Which key words does he clarify at the beginning of the conversation? Which key words does he focus on later in the conversation, and why? You can read the audio script and check your answers on page 156.

Listening is a competence with many dimensions – attitude, knowledge and skills. Many people believe it is the number one success factor for communicating across cultures. As the saying goes: hearing happens, but listening has to be practised. So use the ideas in the engagement process and start practising today.

HOT TIPS

- Show respect for people by giving them your full attention when listening
- Be patient as a listener, especially when listening to people you think have nothing important to say
- Listen for key words used by a speaker and use these same words in your follow-up questions and comments

15 Using questions to listen

By asking effective questions you can achieve most of the ten listening objectives which you read about in Unit 12. But you don't only need to know what questions to ask – you need to know *when* to ask them.

Asking the right question at the right time

Opening

At the beginning of a conversation, effective listeners encourage others with questions. Sometimes the objective is simply to be polite and build rapport, or to get some basic information. At other times it may be to find out how a potential new business partner thinks.

Building rapport	*So when did you arrive?*
	Is this your first time here?
	Can I get you something to drink?
Analysing background	*So do you have much experience of ...?*
	What's your background?
	Have you ever ...?
Understanding attitudes	*What do you think about ...?*
	What's your opinion about ...?
	Do you feel that ...?
Collecting information	(Time) *When	How soon will you finish ...?*
	(Cost) *How much will it cost ...?*
	(Responsibility) *Who's responsible for ...? |*
	Who handles this ...?

Developing

To allow the conversation to develop, effective listeners are able to use a number of different question strategies. In social contexts, they might encourage other people to talk about things which interest them as a way to motivate and please.

Sounds interesting. So tell me a little bit more about ...
So you really had a lot of success. Are you planning to do more?

Alternatively, questions may be selected to influence.

I think we need to do this. What would you think if we ...?
Experience tells me that this is important. How about ...?

Finally, when developing a conversation, effective listeners can ask informal **coaching** questions which encourage the other person to explore their own problem, rather than suggesting solutions too quickly.

Identifying the problem	*What's the problem exactly?*
Investigating the solution	*What have you tried so far to solve the issue?*
	What else could you do?
Setting goals	*So what do you plan to do?*
Planning support	*What kind of support do you think you need?*
Reviewing progress	*When shall we meet to check progress?*

Clarifying

Frequent clarification is extremely important when working across cultures. Remember – never assume you have understood everything correctly.

Clarifying	*Do you mean that ...?*
	*Could you clarify exactly when	what	how	who	why ...?*
	So, if I understand you correctly, ...
	So just to summarise, ...
Confirming	*Why do you say that?*
	What is it you want to achieve, exactly?
	*So your attitude	approach	mindset is ...*
	*So your main concern	worry	motivation	fear	ambition is ...*

As we saw in Unit 14, a great clarification technique is the **keyword approach** – ask speakers to clarify specific words, phrases and sentences.

To clarify data	*You said before that you needed the information urgently. How urgent is 'urgently' exactly? Tomorrow? Next week?*
To clarify feelings	*You said you felt a little disappointed by the results of the survey. Why did you say 'disappointed'?*
To clarify values	*You said that it's important to be honest in discussions. What is 'honest' for you?*

Closing

Effective listeners are good at sensing when a conversation or meeting has come to an end. They use questions to check if the other person is ready to stop, to summarise key actions, and to check on the next meeting. In some cultures it is impolite to end a conversation without a positive reference to the next opportunity to meet.

Ending	*So, shall we finish there?*
	OK, is there anything else?
Summarising	*So, shall I send you ...?*
	So, will you confirm ...?
Future reference	*So, will you be in the office tomorrow?*
	See you next week then?

TRACK 10 Listen to Pilar asking questions in four different situations. At which stage of a conversation is each extract taking place: opening, developing, clarifying or closing? You can read the audio script and check your answers on page 156.

Dialogue 1 ....

Dialogue 2 ....

Dialogue 3 ....

Dialogue 4 ....

Responding to answers

When someone gives us an answer to a question, it's very important to respond effectively as we begin to listen. If we respond badly, a speaker will be less motivated to answer our questions. Let's look at some strategies.

Showing understanding	*I see.	I understand.	OK, I'm with you.*
Showing value	*It's interesting what you say.*
	What you just said is very important, because ...
Sharing experience	*I hear what you're saying. And in my experience ...*
	Yes, in our organisation we find that ...
Building a common platform	*I agree with you about that.*
	Yes, I also think that ...
Empathising	*That must be difficult	interesting	tough.*
	You must have felt ...

Most of us spend too much time telling people things, and not enough time asking them questions and listening to what they say. The next time you open your mouth to say something, remember you have a choice: tell someone something, or ask a question. Most of the time we decide to tell. Try to increase your use of questions and develop your range of responses. You'll find you get better quality information at work and establish better working relationships.

HOT TIPS

- Use questions as a basis for effective listening and conversation management
- Clarify, clarify, and then clarify some more
- Use the keyword approach – ask speakers to explain the meaning of the specific words, phrases and sentences which you don't understand

Getting your message across successfully

'It is impossible to speak in such a way that you cannot be misunderstood.' Karl Popper

Getting your message across successfully in international business is essentially about these three things:

1 You communicate data clearly (people understand what you are communicating)

2 You communicate your intention clearly (people understand why you are communicating)

3 Your communication has the right impact (people feel motivated to act on your message in the way you intended)

As speakers, we have to work very hard – using a number of communication strategies – to make clear not only what we say, so that listeners can understand the basic information we're communicating, but also why we're saying it. If we can do both, there's a greater chance that our communication will have the impact we want, for example people feel comfortable, relaxed, motivated or convinced in some way by our communication.

In this module we examine both principles and techniques to help you get your message across more successfully. We profile your personal communication style to help you understand which people find it easy to listen to you and which people difficult. We focus first on speaking skills, then the module finishes with a look at non-verbal communication.

16 Speaking clearly

17 How to build common understanding

18 Profiling personal communication style

19 Speaking with the right impact

20 Non-verbal communication

16 Speaking clearly

The T-I-P-S model of communication

In order to speak clearly and with the impact we want, we have to consider four things:

T Target

I Information

P Process

S Style

Effective communicators think carefully about both their own needs *and* the needs of the listeners when choosing the **target**, **information**, **process** and **style** for their message. If speakers don't consider the listeners, they risk misinterpretation. They will say things which don't really make sense from the listeners' point of view.

T Target

Is my communication target right for this listener / situation? When you open your mouth to say something, you usually have a purpose for speaking, for example to solve a problem, to give advice or to socialise. However, if the listener has a different sense of purpose about the communication, a different reason for talking to you, miscommunication happens.

🎧 **TRACK 11** Listen to a short extract from a business meeting. What is the chairperson's target for the meeting? What is the objective for the participants? How could the chairperson have avoided this misunderstanding? You can read the audio script and check your answers on page 157.

I Information

Is the information I am communicating right for this listener / situation? It's generally true that individuals prefer to talk about what they know and what's important to them, which is often less known and less important to others. When working across cultures, there is the added problem that people think about information very differently. For some, high complexity, sophisticated analysis and attention to detail mean professionalism. To others, this can mean information overload, and unnecessary discussion of facts and figures causing delays in decision-making. Choosing which information to talk about and to which level of detail, therefore, can be a difficult task.

TRACK 12   Listen to a short extract from a dinner conversation. How successful is Pierre in selecting the right topic and the right level of detail? You can read the audio script and check your answers on page 157.

P   Process

Is the communication process right for the listener / situation? In international business everyone would say that they understand the terms *email, telephone conference, meeting, presentation,* and so on. The problem is that across cultures and between personalities the interpretation of these terms can differ enormously. A meeting can be for top-down briefings in one culture but for direct and open discussions in another culture. A presentation may be an explanation of facts for some, but for others it may be an opportunity for entertainment and self-marketing.

Communication becomes unclear and problematic across cultures when professionals force their own assumptions about these communication processes on others – they argue in a meeting when others would agree in public, only to negotiate privately later; or they send an email to resolve a conflict when others would telephone.

You will communicate more clearly across cultures if you clarify the process of communication events.

TRACK 13   Listen to a short extract from the beginning of a negotiation between Klaus and Peter. How does Klaus clarify the negotiation process? How successful is he with this approach? You can read the audio script and check your answers on page 157.

S   Style

Is my communication style right for the listener / situation? Our communication style is influenced by our personality and the various cultural groups we belong to – national, company, family. This style will be clear to some and have a positive impact. For others, however, it will be confusing, perhaps even unprofessional, and have a negative impact.

You will communicate more clearly across cultures if you understand and manage your own communication style.

Effective communicators can profile their communication style in three dimensions:

– **physical** (channel): do I speak at the right speed and with the right volume?

– **pragmatic** (data): am I too complex or too simple, am I too analytical or too results-oriented?

– **psychological** (relationship): am I too friendly or too reserved, am I too extroverted or too introverted?

🔊 TRACK 14   Listen to a short extract from a telephone call. Why do John and Jim have problems understanding each other? Who is responsible for the misunderstanding? How could it have been avoided? You can read the audio script and check your answers on pages 157–8.

So in the future, think strategically about why, what and how you communicate. Think about your audiences' expectations of target, information, process and style before and while you communicate with them. Then you can align your message to their interests and create the right impact.

HOT TIPS

- Think before you speak – plan how to communicate in a way which makes sense to the listener
- Monitor how listeners respond to you during conversations to see how effectively you are communicating to them
- Change your normal communication habits if you think they will create misunderstanding in the mind of the listener

17 How to build common understanding

Here are five techniques for clear communication you can use in your professional working life to build common understanding.

1 Communicate the background context and positive motivation behind your message

Remember the iceberg model of communication from Unit 4? I can hear *what* you say, but I can't see inside your head to know *why* you said it. Clear communicators give background information about what they're saying *and* make sure that the listener understands that the message has a positive intention.

🎧 TRACK 15   Listen to an extract from a telephone call. How does John misunderstand Sabine?

🎧 TRACK 16   Now listen to a second version of the same telephone call in which Sabine communicates more clearly and successfully. What does she say at the beginning of the call to create a positive impression? Which background information does Sabine then give to explain her request? You can read the audio scripts and check your answers on page 158.

2 Say what you are *not* saying before you say what you want to say

In the first call Sabine makes, she has to apologise and explain to John that she was not criticising him. Although the apology may be effective, clear communicators should be proactive and avoid the need for this kind of apology. They can do this by stating explicitly what they are *not* saying before they actually communicate the main message. This makes the message much clearer.

🎧 TRACK 17   Listen to an extract from a presentation. What does the presenter state explicitly is *not* her objective? What does she then present as her actual objective? You can read the audio script and check your answers on page 158.

Not the objective: ....

Actual objective: ....

3 KISSSSS – Keep it Short, Simple, Structured, Slow and the Same

Clearly, speakers who construct long and complex messages and who speak without enough structure are more difficult to follow, particularly in a foreign language. These speakers become even more difficult to understand if they talk too quickly and if they only give the key message once.

🎧 TRACK 18   Listen to an extract from a video conference meeting. How effective do you think Paul is as an international communicator? What three suggestions does Sophie make to Paul? You can read the audio script and check your answers on page 158.

Suggestion 1   ....

Suggestion 2   ....

Suggestion 3   ....

4 Give listeners an opportunity to clarify

Effective speakers can help a listener to understand by giving them regular opportunities to clarify or comment on what has been said – to become a full partner in the communication. This creates a **positive loop** which makes it easier to build common understanding.

 TRACK 19   Listen to an extract from a negotiation between Dirk, a purchaser, and Simone, a supplier. What two questions does Dirk ask Simone to support clear communication? What point is clarified as a result of the second question? You can read the audio script and check your answers on page 158.

Question 1 ....

Question 2 ....

Point clarified ....

5 Make time for more communication

It takes time to communicate clearly when working internationally. If you don't allow enough time, communication will suffer.

Take time before meetings, presentations and negotiations to think about objectives. Network with key people to find out their opinions and to get the necessary background information before you meet.

Take time during the meeting or negotiation to write down what was discussed or agreed. Don't rely only on the spoken word, because language is sometimes a poor vehicle for communication.

Take time to ask for feedback at the end – how could we do it better next time? Communicate about how to communicate better!

Take time after the meeting or negotiation to confirm understanding or engagement with the results. Ask for feedback again in private for ideas on how to make communication clearer.

HOT TIPS

- Make sure the listener understands the positive motivation behind your message
- Create common understanding by asking the listener to comment on what you say
- Allow more time for communication when working internationally

18 Profiling personal communication style

Some interculturalists try to describe the communication styles of national business cultures and identify the risks to clarity and impact caused by different values, attitudes and habits. For example, in his book *Understanding American and German Business Culures*, Patrick Schmidt contrasts what he sees as features of German and American styles across several dimensions.

Contrasting German and American communication styles

German	American
complicated	simple
thoughtful	fast
detailed	concise
analytical	sloganistic
formal	informal
serious	humorous
excellent listeners	easily bored
factual	exaggerated
reserved	personal
direct and serious	direct and friendly

This comparison highlights the potential risk for a breakdown in communication as a result of different communication styles.

What is your communication style?

Generalisations or stereotypes at the level of national culture can provide an interesting if sometimes dangerous platform for reflection and discussion. However, it is more important to understand your own personal style and to reflect how it can affect the clarity and impact of your own communication with your specific business partners.

As individuals we each have a personal communication style. We communicate the *what* and the *why* in different ways for both psychological and cultural reasons. These different styles affect the clarity and impact of our communication for those listening to us.

Here is a quick and informal personal profiling process (in five steps) using a checklist. Of course, it isn't pure science, but just completing this five-step process will make you think more carefully about how you communicate internationally and help you to identify how you can improve your clarity and impact.

Personal communication style – profile

1 Circle the word in each pairing below which most correctly describes your style.

	Fast speaker	**Slow speaker**
Physical	loud	quiet
	energetic	calm
	touching	distant
	smiling	serious
Informational	long and complex	short and simple
	analytical	results-oriented
	structured	flexible
	direct	indirect
	time-focused	time-relaxed
Psychological	introverted	extroverted
	impersonal	personal
	open	closed
	emotional	neutral
	pushing	helping

2 Now ask a colleague if he or she agrees with your self-evaluation. And revise it accordingly.

3 Next, analyse how your international partners will see your style – both the positives and the negatives.

4 Plan a communication style strategy for your next communication event – meeting, presentation or negotiation – in line with the results of point 3.

5 After the event, get feedback from your audience on your communication style. Were you clear? Did you have a positive / negative impact? Decide which areas you need to continue to improve.

HOT TIPS

- Become more aware of your typical communication behaviours
- Understand which audiences will judge your style positively and which more negatively
- Use feedback as a tool for developing your range of communication styles

19 Speaking with the right impact

In any business context we want what we say to have the right impact. In this unit we look at ways to persuade and convince more successfully.

The psychology of persuasion

Robert Cialdini in his book *Influence: The Psychology of Persuasion* describes six fundamental persuasion principles for communicators.

1 **Authority**
People are more likely to do something or accept an idea if the ideas are communicated or validated by a person in a position of power.
Sorry, but the CEO needs the information now!

2 **Liking**
People are more likely to do something or accept an idea if the ideas are communicated by someone they like.
Could you do it for me? Just for me, please?

3 **Social proof**
People are more likely to do something or accept an idea if the ideas are accepted or followed by lots of other people.
Everybody else around the table agrees. Peter, can I come to you, finally? What do you think?

4 **Exclusivity**
People are more likely to do something or accept an idea if what is offered is in some way a 'special deal'.
OK. We don't offer this level of discount for anyone else but I can make an exception for you: 50%. OK? We have a deal?

5 **Reciprocation**
People are more likely to do something or accept an idea if the person making the suggestion has previously done something for them.
Look, I accepted your proposed changes on the technical platform. Can you accept my changes on pricing?

6 **Consistency**
People are more likely to do something or accept an idea if it is consistent with something they are doing already and / or did in the past.
Look, does anyone disagree with these changes? I mean, in many ways we're simply extending things we already have in place at the moment – but in a way which helps us to save costs. So I don't really see any issue at all.

Interestingly, Cialdini sees these principles as human universals and doesn't investigate the cultural dynamics of his principles in great detail. However, it could be, for example, that the **authority** principle is used more frequently in top-down business cultures. It may be that the **liking** principle is used more frequently in more relationship-driven cultures. Communicating across cultures needs careful selection of the right principle for the right context.

TRACK 20   Now listen to two business conversations. Identify which of Cialdini's influencing principles are used in each one. You can read the audio script and check your answers on page 159.

Conversation 1   ....

Conversation 2   ....

More ideas on how to improve the impact of your message

Here are some more ideas about persuasion and creating convincing messages which have an impact. Which do you agree with?

Logic   'At the end of the day, people are convinced by good arguments and solid data.'

Benefit   'People are more likely to be influenced if someone communicates clear benefits. Interestingly, we may influence less by telling people what they need but more by asking people what they want, and then delivering solutions to satisfy this want.'

Passion   'In my culture you have to communicate with a lot of energy and passion if you want to influence. But I know that in other places people respond to a quieter, more reflective and analytical style.'

Honesty   'People who come across as open and honest are more likely to win commitment. People who keep things back, who play tactical, are not credible.'

Vision   'People who have a clear vision of the future, who know what they want and how to get there, are more engaging and influential.'

Positivity   'Negative people will never be successful here. Positive and enthusiastic thinkers dedicated to finding creative solutions are more appealing.'

Conviction   If someone isn't convinced by their own argument, they'll never convince anyone else.

Trust   'People will only be influenced by those they trust. There are a number of trust factors, but in my business culture trust depends almost 100% on believing people have the right competence.'

Which of the strategies could you use in your work?

For more ideas on how to influence, see Unit 35 *Influencing people in your network* and Unit 45 *Building trust across cultures*

HOT TIPS

- Prepare persuasion strategies which are tailored to the specific individual and cultural context
- Take time after presentations and meetings to evaluate how successful you are in convincing people

20 Non-verbal communication

It is often said that we communicate meaning more with our facial expression, our gestures and the way we say something than with what we actually say. Here we look at four dimensions of non-verbal communication.

1 Appearance – body and clothing

The moment people see you, they begin to make assessments about you based on how you look – your physique, your height, your skin colour, your hairstyle, your clothing.

Clothing communicates powerful messages. Roles in societies everywhere are defined by the use of uniforms, for example policemen and nurses. In business we also have uniforms – suits and ties for men, for example.

Ask yourself:

– In what ways does your appearance reflect your cultural and individual identity?
– What impact does your appearance have on your international business partners?
– How could you adapt your appearance generally to create a better impact on those from other cultures?

2 Physical environment

The architecture of an office, the style and organisation of the furniture in it, the general decoration – all these are things organisations use to communicate and support key cultural values such as tradition, modernity, fun, creativity; and to create a mindset and support types of communication behaviour in their staff.

Personal space concerns the way people think about and use the physical area around them. In some organisational cultures, it's acceptable to mark private office space with a closed door. In others the boundary must be left open, because it communicates a sense of openness and collaboration.

Cultures also differ enormously in attitudes to how close people can stand to each other and how much the boundary can be broken with touching.

Ask yourself:

– What cultural values does your organisational environment communicate?
– What cultural values do the organisational environments of your business partners communicate?
– How much space do you typically have between yourself and another person when standing and talking? For which international partners might this be uncomfortable?

3 Body language

When we talk about body language, we mean the following things.

* body posture – how we stand, face other people, sit, and position our hands
* facial expression – smiling, mouth open, eyes closed, and so on
* gestures – pointing, closed fist, thumbs up, and so on

Related areas are the study of touching and the study of eye contact.

The main challenge across cultures is to interpret other people's body language correctly, especially when similar gestures or facial expressions, for example, may have very different meanings.

Smiling is a classic example. In some cultural contexts it can indicate friendliness, in others nervousness. It may even be interpreted as a lack of seriousness and professionalism. Similarly, with eye contact – is strong eye contact a sign of positive engagement, or a sign of hostility? It depends where you are in the world.

The second challenge is to ensure that people get a positive impression from your body language. In business meetings, for example, this might mean that you concentrate on leaning forward on the desk, or make eye contact with participants regularly to show engagement and willingness to share ideas.

Wherever you are in the world, you risk generating a negative impression by leaning back in your seat, yawning and looking at the ceiling, or looking out of the window.

One area of study, neuro-linguistic programming, suggests 'mirroring' is the safest strategy. Mirroring means that you observe very closely the body language of your partner and become a mirror image – not to copy and to mimic, but simply to make the other person feel comfortable and to minimise the risk of misinterpretation of your 'strange' movements.

Ask yourself:

– How would you describe your typical body language during a meeting, or when giving a professional presentation?
– Which aspects of your body language might be confusing or irritating for your international partners?

4 Paralinguistics

There is a saying: *It's not so much* **what** *you say, but* **how** *you say it that matters* – and this is what **paralinguistics** is. There are a number of key dimensions which can significantly change the way in which words and sentences are understood in different cultures and by different individuals.

Speed	Some people may think fast speakers are more competent.
Volume	Some people may think loud speakers are arrogant.
Tone	Some people may think a soft tone shows openness to others.
Pitch	Some people may think speakers with lower pitch are stronger or more mature.
Fill	Some people may think people who use sounds like 'uh', or give little laughs, are nervous or unsure.
Quality	Some people may think speakers who articulate well and have a smooth rhythm are more educated and competent.

Ask yourself:

– What impact does your voice have on your business partners?
– What impressions and assumptions might it generate?
– Which of the paralinguistic dimensions above would it be useful for you to improve?

Managing non-verbal communication – five things to remember

1 We often unconsciously evaluate the non-verbal communication of other people, and then make very important judgements (positive and negative) about their professional expertise, their personality and what they might think about us.

2 We often communicate these judgements to other people without realising it through our own non-verbal communication. For example, you might smile at someone you like, or reduce eye contact with someone you don't respect. It's important to realise that even if you don't actually *say* negative or positive things about a person, you may still communicate it non-verbally.

3 We need to manage our non-verbal communication consciously. As we become aware of our feelings, we should change what we're doing. For example, if you're feeling bored, you may be sitting back in your chair. When you realise this is happening, you could lean forward in your chair and re-establish eye contact.

4 We need to observe very closely the non-verbal communication of others. If you see a problem – for example, the other person looks angry or bored – you can ask a question to check everything is OK.

5 Non-verbal communication is open to the same process of misinterpretation as verbal communication. We will misinterpret other people's, and they will misinterpret ours. Only with a great deal of experience and practice are we able to analyse the behaviours of others accurately.

HOT TIPS

- Manage your non-verbal communication to create a positive impact on your communication partners
- Observe others closely to check how far they are engaged during the communication process
- Use questions to confirm how other people are thinking and feeling, particularly if you think you see that someone is feeling uncomfortable or has another opinion during a discussion

Communicating for international business – 1

'The single biggest problem in communication is the illusion that it has taken place.' George Bernard Shaw

At a recent international meeting the discussion focused on how to solve a difficult IT problem. Five minutes into the meeting, it was quite clear that something was wrong.

Some members of the audience – possibly from a more hierarchical business culture – were saying very little. They expected to be informed by the leader of the meeting about the solution he had found. In fact, they expected a presentation rather than a discussion.

Others in the meeting were saying a lot and discussing the issue energetically and in great detail. Indeed, their discussion sounded almost like an argument.

A few people at the back of the room were using the meeting as an opportunity to chat to colleagues they hadn't seen for a long time and to exchange important company gossip.

How familiar does this situation sound to you? One of the major challenges with business communication across cultures is that people view meetings or presentations in very different ways.

To manage these different expectations effectively and to reach goals efficiently, you need to develop a flexible approach to these 'moments of communication'. You need an approach which enables information to flow and people to interact effectively. This module provides some tips and tools to support you in presentations and meetings.

21 International presentations – knowing your audience

22 International presentations – the art of answering questions

23 International meetings – getting it right from the start

24 International meetings – managing the discussion

25 International meetings – making a decision and closing

21 International presentations – knowing your audience

People can have very different ideas about what makes a good presentation. So it's very important that you find out about your audience's expectations *before* you give your presentation. You can then use this information during your presentation to engage your audience as much as possible.

Here are nine key questions to answer before your next presentation.

1 How will my presentation benefit the audience?

Audiences need to understand the benefits of listening to your presentation. Make it very clear in your introduction why people should listen to you.

What I want to do today is look at how we can improve our global talent programme. I know this is important to you because all of you have to sponsor your best people in this process

2 What is the role of the audience? Should people listen silently or be active participants?

Some audiences listen in silence as a sign of respect to the presenter, and in order to concentrate. They expect questions will come at the end. However, many presenters like to ask audiences to interact during their presentation.

I'd really like to hear your views and questions during the presentation.
I'd prefer today to be a dialogue rather than a monologue.

3 What is my role as presenter? Am I expected to be an expert with all the answers?

It's useful to clarify your role explicitly, particularly if you are *not* in the position of expert.

I'd like to clarify at the beginning my role here. I don't see myself as the expert. But I am someone who can help you, the experts, solve the problems.

4 How far should I focus my presentation on action (what has been done and what is to do) or analysis (what is known and what is to find out)?

Attitudes to 'analysis' and 'action' can differ significantly across the cultures of both countries and organisations. In financial services organisations, for example, detailed analysis is seen as a form of professional risk management. On the other hand, in retail organisations which are future-oriented and customer-focused, this approach would be far too slow. You need to find out what the expectation is: action or analysis?

5 What is my audience's attitude to structure and organisation?

In some contexts a very clearly-signposted presentation is seen as evidence of good planning and professionalism. In other contexts, it could show a lack of imagination and an inability to think creatively.

6 How much time should I spend at the beginning on a personal introduction?

This depends on whether the context is relationship-oriented or task-oriented. Task-oriented audiences want a focus on professional responsibility. Relationship-oriented audiences like to hear more private details beyond job titles.

I'm Head of Quality in the company and head of a family of three boys at home!

7 How far does my audience expect information? How far is entertainment demanded?

This is a question about style. In some business cultures a presentation is a performance, with the presenter entertaining the audience with humour, fun and lots of charisma. In other contexts, in front of an audience which just wants hard data delivered without any show, this approach can fail.

8 How good is the English of my audience?

If key members of your audience have a poor level of English, you'll need to support them in a number of ways, for example with an interpreter, with translated handouts, with handouts written in simple English and / or by speaking more slowly, repeating important messages and allowing plenty of time for clarification and discussion.

9 Which decisions will my presentation support? Who is the decision-maker?

Presentations often support a decision-making process. In this situation it's vital you identify the key decision-maker(s) in the audience. You also need to find out how quickly decisions will be made. Will they be made at the presentation or later?

TRACK 21   Now listen to two short extracts from the beginning of two presentations and say which statement is correct (*Yes* or *No*) for each. You can read the audio script and check your answers on page 159.

	Presentation 1	Presentation 2
1 The benefit is clearly stated.	Yes	....
2 The presenter role is expert.	....	....
3 The audience role is to be interactive.	....	....
4 The focus is on action.	....	....

Culture strategy

In the second extract, the presenter asks his audience members to take a role which is not typical in their culture. What do you think of this strategy for an international presenter? Check your answers on page 159.

HOT TIPS

- Know each of your audience's expectations of 'a good presentation'
- Deliver content in a style which matches these expectations and reaches your objectives
- Make it possible for people to understand you – speak slowly, use clear English, give handouts, allow enough opportunities for reflection and clarification

22 International presentations – the art of answering questions

Providing time for questions is a vital part of the presentation process. As presenter, you need to create a communication loop with questions and answers to support clear and effective transfer of information, *particularly* for audiences working in a second language. Develop a presentation culture of questioning by implementing the following five-step process both during and at the end of a presentation.

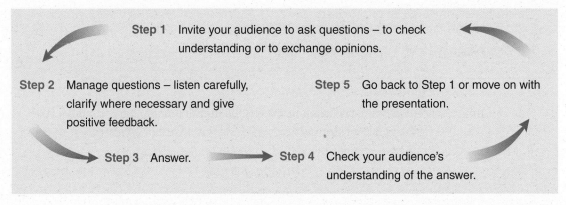

Step 1 Invite your audience to ask questions – to check understanding or to exchange opinions.

Step 2 Manage questions – listen carefully, clarify where necessary and give positive feedback.

Step 5 Go back to Step 1 or move on with the presentation.

Step 3 Answer.

Step 4 Check your audience's understanding of the answer.

🌐 **TRACK 22**   Listen and read the following extract from a presentation. Underline the words which the speaker uses to complete steps 1, 2, 4 and 5. Check your answers on pages 159–60.

Speaker   OK. I'm sure that there'll be questions about this so let me stop there for a second. *(pause)* John, do you have any comments? You told me that you were a little unsure before I started?

John   Yes, I was. I'm still a little unsure, particularly about the costings for the project. You didn't mention exact figures. When will we have this data?

Speaker   You mean the data for the whole project, or the pilot?

John   Both.

Speaker   OK, it's a good question. Perhaps I wasn't very clear. The pilot costs are available in the back of your handout – that's the €2.5m estimate. The total project costing depends on some figures from our external consultants. But I will let you have that by the end of the week. OK?

John   Fine. That's clear.

Speaker   Right, let's now turn to marketing.

Many presenters like to give positive feedback with phrases like *That's a good question* to the audience. In your working contexts, when could it have a positive effect, and when might it have a negative effect? For example, some audiences may think you are not being honest if you overuse it.

How questions can help the presenter convince an audience

Effective presenters can use the five-step process to check to see if members of the audience agree with their message. If people express disagreement, the presenter can develop arguments in their answers to convince the audience.

TRACK 23   Listen and read another extract from a presentation and again underline the words which the speaker uses to complete steps 1, 2, 4 and 5. Check your answers on page 160

Speaker   OK. I know this represents a significant change and you'll need to clarify the impact on your local organisations. Are there any questions about this or comments so far?

Eva   To be honest, I still don't see the benefits to us locally. We have an efficient IT system already and the new system is only going to make things more complex.

Speaker   Good. I think that's a critical question because we all need to be very clear about why we're doing this. Firstly, Eva, I need you to think not only with a local mindset but also with a new regional mindset. This is a process to create a standard for the whole of the region which will mean that we can run our whole business better. We need to think together and not alone. I think it's clear that a single system brings less complexity and less cost for the whole of the business – instead of ten systems to manage we have one. Can you see that?

Eva   Yes, of course.

Speaker   Good. I think once the principles are clear, we can move forward to look at the details. But I will stress again, we need a new mindset for the future. We have to say goodbye to local thinking ... and I'll visit each of your offices with this message in the coming months. So, any more questions about complexity or can we move on?

The presenter tells Eva very clearly in front of others that her way of thinking is not correct for this situation. In some cultural contexts this will be too direct and insensitive towards Eva. How far would it be possible in your working contexts to handle the question in this way?

Dealing with audiences that don't ask questions

As we saw in Unit 21, audiences may be reluctant to ask questions for a variety of reasons. They may be worried about their level of English or asking questions may go against certain cultural norms. However, it could still be your objective to create a dialogue with your audience if you feel this is important to support their understanding. In these situations it's a good idea to have question prompts or questions prepared. Here is an example:

Presenter   Are there any questions about choosing suppliers before I move on?

Audience   (*Silence*)

Presenter   Well, one question I'm often asked is about the tendering process for suppliers. I usually recommend …

Having prepared questions will encourage the audience to start asking questions themselves.

Dealing with questions you can't answer

You may be worried you won't be able to answer all the audience's questions. Perhaps someone's question will raise an issue you don't want raised!

Stay positive at all times. Difficult or 'wrong' questions can be useful, even when they're challenging you. It's an opportunity for the presenter to learn the different opinions and perspectives of people from other cultural backgrounds. Even questions which criticise directly may deliver an opportunity to restate something in a memorable way.

🔊 TRACK 24   Listen to an extract from a presentation where the presenter takes the opportunity to emphasise a key point again. You can read the audio script on page 160.

Lastly, you may not have enough time to answer all the audience's questions, particularly in contexts where asking a lot of questions is normal. In this situation it's important that you note down any unanswered questions and promise to answer by email or over the phone.

HOT TIPS

- Invite questions as a way to clarify levels of understanding and acceptance
- View critical questions as an opportunity to hear diverse opinions and to repeat your key arguments
- Be sensitive to the fact that in some cultures audiences will find it challenging to ask questions openly, and may be sensitive to direct answers

23 International meetings – getting it right from the start

The culture of meetings can vary significantly from country to country, from company to company, even from department to department. To create an effective meeting culture for your international department, team or network, you need to think about the four Ps: purpose, people, place and process.

Purpose

Across cultures there can be very different expectations about the purpose of a meeting. Is the meeting to inform, to brief, to discuss, to decide, to brainstorm, to socialise, to complain or to look to the future?

In more hierarchical working cultures the meeting may just be a briefing from the boss with no opportunity for discussion. In more creative cultural contexts, such as marketing firms, the generation of ideas may be normal.

One way to manage these different expectations is to openly **surface** them, propose a solution to **satisfy** the various points of view, and then **suggest** your objective for the meeting.

Listen and read this example. Underline the language which the chair uses to surface, satisfy and suggest. Check your answers on page 160.

🌐 **TRACK 25**

Chair   OK, the purpose of today's meeting is to decide on the next steps for the IT project which is now a little behind schedule. I know that some of you would like to discuss these problems and the reasons for them in detail but I really want this meeting to focus just on what we need to do in the next two weeks to get things back on track a little. We'll find time next week to analyse the causes of the problems in more detail but I would like to focus on next steps today. Is that OK with everyone?

How far could you use the **surface** – **satisfy** – **suggest** approach in your meetings?

People

You need to think carefully about who will be at the meeting. Will all the key stakeholders be there? Is it better for senior management *not* to attend in order that a team can make progress on its own? What kind of minutes will be needed to report back after the meeting to stakeholders who are not at the meeting?

You'll probably need to do a lot of networking to persuade key people with very busy schedules to attend: *I think it's really important you attend this meeting, because without you we can't really move the project forward.*

Place

In a multinational context the place for the meeting is a key factor. Don't make the mistake of holding all international meetings at the headquarters. Rotating meetings between local offices can have real motivational and team-building outcomes for international groups.

Process

How the meeting will be managed is as important as its purpose. For many, setting and following a strict agenda is the way to structure and manage a meeting. It enables clear objectives to be defined and roles to be allocated.

For key meetings, telephone participants to confirm their agreement with the agenda and to discuss general expectations of the meeting. This pre-meeting contact can 'manage' disagreements, confusions or hidden agendas and will enable the meeting to be more productive when people get together face-to-face.

But be careful with agendas. Some people may see focusing on the agenda as too formal and mechanistic; they may even view an agenda as a technique to control them.

🌐 **TRACK 26**   With these diverse expectations it can be very important to set ground rules for a meeting. Listen to the start of a meeting. What do you think of Peter's approach as chair? You can read the audio script on page 160.

In the extract Peter mentions the common rules which everyone has agreed as a way to make their meetings more effective. Creating communication ground rules is a recognised way to manage cultural diversity. If people buy into this, it can work.

Which five useful ground rules could you set for *your* international meetings which would make them more efficient?

Remember, in some cultural contexts setting rules in this way may not feel comfortable for some people. However, discussing rules, even if you decide not to fix any, will clarify different expectations and support better communication.

HOT TIPS

- Telephone key participants in advance of a meeting to clarify their expectations and to confirm the agenda for the meeting
- Consider the political landscape around the meeting when planning where and when to hold the meeting and who to invite
- Agree the ground rules for good communication at the start

24 International meetings – managing the discussion

The way people interact in meetings varies greatly across cultures. Some may want to speak without interruption for a long time, whereas others will expect interruption and a quick exchange of ideas or points of view. Also, when people disagree with each other, they may be direct or indirect in the way they give their opinion. Here we explore how to handle these differences in style.

Speaking-listening styles

When people interact, two obvious things happen: one person speaks, the other person listens. And then the roles change as the listener begins to speak and the first speaker listens.

Look at how different people describe their own speaking and listening styles in meetings. Which of these descriptions is similar to your own style?

Speaking styles

'I try not to speak too much because I don't want to dominate.'

'I just keep talking. If people want to stop me, they have to interrupt me. And that's OK with me. I like interruptions. For me, it shows people care about what I say.'

'I like structured discussions where each individual says their opinions one by one. And I prefer to give full and detailed explanations when I speak. I think this is professional.'

'I expect people to listen to me in silence. I hate it when people interrupt.'

'When I speak, I try to be very precise and focused so that people can understand me easily. After speaking, I usually then involve and engage the listener in some way, maybe with a question like *What do you think?*'

Listening styles

'I listen in silence. I just concentrate on understanding the other person.'

'In smaller meetings, I like to make comments as I listen like *Interesting.* or *Really?* to show interest in what the speaker is saying.'

'I ask a lot of questions when I listen to check I have really understood.'

'Sometimes I'm not very patient and I interrupt, especially if the speaker is talking and talking and not really saying anything.'

'I never interrupt people. It's just rude!'

🔊 **TRACK 27** Listen to an extract from a meeting between Dirk, Per-Erik and Danielle. Match the people with the speaking-listening styles below.

1 Per-Erik .....   2 Danielle .....   3 Dirk .....

a Interrupts when listening, sometimes to agree with the speaker and confirm what was said, but also to disagree and introduce a new point. Does not speak for a long time. Likes asking questions.

b Speaks in a structured way. Likes to develop logical arguments which take time to explain. Does not interrupt others when they are speaking.

c Says very little. For this person listening means asking questions to clarify or investigate the other person's ideas.

What do you think Dirk might feel about Danielle's communication style in the meeting? You can read the audio script and check your answers on pages 160–1.

Which of these speaking and listening styles do you think is the best for *your* international meetings?

The Positive Interactive Approach

The Positive Interactive Approach (PIA) is a discussion style for international meetings. It aims to proactively manage the interaction between speaker and listener. The PIA speaking and listening style generates a form of communication in meetings which supports common understanding and builds positive relationships. The strategies for Person 1 (black) and Person 2 (brown) are explained in the graphic below:

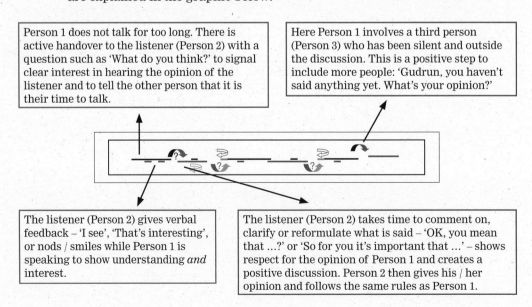

Person 1 does not talk for too long. There is active handover to the listener (Person 2) with a question such as 'What do you think?' to signal clear interest in hearing the opinion of the listener and to tell the other person that it is their time to talk.

Here Person 1 involves a third person (Person 3) who has been silent and outside the discussion. This is a positive step to include more people: 'Gudrun, you haven't said anything yet. What's your opinion?'

The listener (Person 2) gives verbal feedback – 'I see', 'That's interesting', or nods / smiles while Person 1 is speaking to show understanding *and* interest.

The listener (Person 2) takes time to comment on, clarify or reformulate what is said – 'OK, you mean that ...?' or 'So for you it's important that ...' – shows respect for the opinion of Person 1 and creates a positive discussion. Person 2 then gives his / her opinion and follows the same rules as Person 1.

TRACK 28 Now listen to an extract from another meeting in which Nicola and Serge use the Positive Interactive Approach with each other. How far could you use it in your international meetings? You can read the audio script on page 161.

Disagreement styles

 TRACK 29 A major cause of misunderstandings in meetings is different styles of disagreement. Listen to this extract from a meeting. How effective do you think Hans's style of disagreement is in the context of this meeting? You can read the audio script and check your answers on page 161.

Styles of disagreement differ across cultures. In some contexts direct disagreement is seen as efficient, truthful and objective-oriented. For individuals from cultures very sensitive to personal feeling and public face, directness may be a source of conflict. Of course, indirectness may also cause problems for individuals who value more direct forms of disagreement. Look at the contrast of styles below and how people may see each other.

> Person A may feel Person B is superficial, not competent or convinced of own ideas, is playing games and cannot be trusted

Person A (disagrees directly)
I prefer to be honest with others and I like to state my opinions openly. I think it's more efficient to do it this way than trying to be too polite. I think if you believe in something, say it strongly.

Person B (disagrees indirectly)
I prefer to keep a positive atmosphere in the meeting and to avoid any bad feeling between people by attacking them in any way. I like to focus on the positive in other people's ideas, even if I disagree with them.

> Person B may feel Person A is inflexible, arrogant, impolite, focused on self-interest, not a team player.

Remember, there is no single or perfect solution to business communication in terms of speaking-listening or disagreement style. Culturally-intelligent managers should simply assess their cultural contexts and use the style which is right for the specific situation.

HOT TIPS

- Observe and analyse the speaking-listening style (and disagreement style) of people you have meetings with
- Use a communication style which is acceptable for others
- Implement the Positive Interactive Approach when it helps in a meeting
- Discuss differences in style openly so that everyone can understand each other's way of communicating in meetings

25 International meetings – making a decision and closing

There are a number of things which affect decision-making in international meetings:

Responsibility   In top-down hierarchical business cultures, authority for making decisions will be in the hands of senior management only. In flatter business cultures many people will give their opinions and take part in the decision-making process.

Speed   In some business cultures decisions are taken slowly using in-depth analysis of detailed information. In other contexts people may take decisions quickly and then adapt later if changes are necessary.

Commitment   Internationally, the commitment behind decisions or agreements may vary. In some cultures a verbal promise is final and binding. In other cultures even written agreements may be seen as flexible and open to change as more people are consulted and / or circumstances change.

Making decisions in international meetings

If you're leading the meeting, it's very important to focus people on reaching an agreement before their planes take them back home. There are three stages to this focusing process:

1 **Push** the group to a decision
2 **Confirm** the decision
3 **Clarify** who's responsible for implementing the decision, and by when

🎧 **TRACK 30**   Listen to an extract from a meeting where the chairperson, Maria, uses this technique to take a decision. In what cultural contexts might this approach be problematic? You can read the audio script and check your answers on page 161.

Closing an international meeting

Often at the end of an international meeting people are not sure about what exactly has been agreed. If this is the case, they may be too embarrassed to say so! Here is a seven-step process for closing international meetings.

1 Check that there are no further items to discuss, or further comments
2 Summarise the meeting: review objectives and decisions
3 Ensure that everyone understands the decisions taken

4 Clarify responsibilities for any actions, including circulation of minutes

5 Arrange a date for the next meeting

6 Focus on the positive results of the meeting and thank people for their contributions

7 End the meeting formally

🎧 **TRACK 31** Listen to an extract from the close of a meeting. Which of the seven steps does the chairperson *not* include? You can read the audio script and check your answer on pages 161–2.

In the extract, the chair explicitly celebrates the success of the meeting. How important in your working context is it to 'celebrate success' in this way at the end of important meetings?

Don't think decision-making ends when the meeting ends. Effective international managers network with participants of their meeting by telephone after the event to confirm again understanding of decisions and their commitment to the agreed actions. Without such motivational networking, implementation of actions often falls behind schedule as participants give time to other priorities.

HOT TIPS

- Understand the different decision-making styles of key individuals in your international meetings
- Get to a decision faster by using the focusing process of **Push**, **Confirm** and **Clarify**
- Close the meeting with an explicit summary of decisions and schedule of actions

Communicating for international business – 2

'Communication works for those who work at it.'   John Powell

This module focuses on two areas of business communication which can be very challenging: 'virtual' working via email and telephone, and negotiating across cultures.

We look at how to communicate your email messages clearly and how to avoid misunderstandings.

We examine the advantages of using the telephone to communicate, and give tips on managing your phone calls.

Unit 28 on telephone conferencing develops the work you have already done on meetings, but also gives you tips on how to handle difficult virtual meetings via telephone.

Finally, we look at how people across cultures understand the meaning and purpose of negotiation differently. We then go on to examine strategies to manage these differences within your international negotiations.

26 International emailing

The large number of emails we receive from colleagues, customers and suppliers creates pressure for us all. The danger is that under pressure we send emails which are unclear or which contain mistakes, and that generates even more work for us and the person we've emailed. Here are some ideas for managing email effectively.

Tips for writing better emails across cultures

Tip 1 Before sending any email, ask yourself whether a telephone call is a better option. It may even be better to meet in person, particularly if you need to deal with differences of opinion or conflicts. Compare these two examples.

High-risk communication: negative tone email, no telephone call

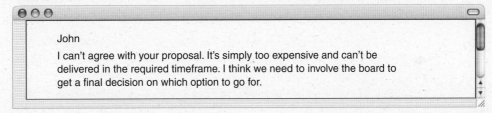

John

I can't agree with your proposal. It's simply too expensive and can't be delivered in the required timeframe. I think we need to involve the board to get a final decision on which option to go for.

Low-risk communication: positive tone email plus telephone call

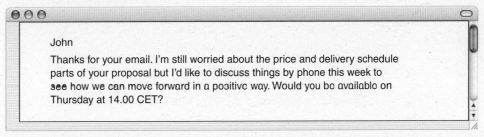

John

Thanks for your email. I'm still worried about the price and delivery schedule parts of your proposal but I'd like to discuss things by phone this week to see how we can move forward in a positive way. Would you be available on Thursday at 14.00 CET?

Tip 2 Nobody wants to spend time reading emails which are poorly structured or difficult to read. Use these ideas to keep your emails reader-friendly.

– Create a clear and explicit subject head for the email.
– Avoid complex vocabulary, long sentences and too many direct questions which are difficult to answer.
– Structure ideas into separate paragraphs which makes them easier to reply to.
– Limit the number of topics you deal with in a single email.

Read through the last three emails which you sent. How many of the guidelines above did they follow?

Tip 3 Information is valued across cultures in different ways. There are cultures where it's the norm to provide a lot of information with a great level of detail on a regular and frequent basis, perhaps in an informal conversational style. On the other hand, there are cultures which require less information, with less quality, much less often and much more directly. Compare these two examples.

This is what the email said:

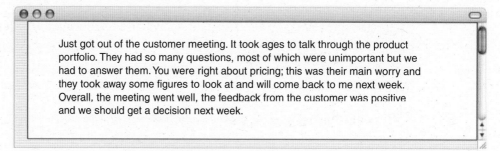

Just got out of the customer meeting. It took ages to talk through the product portfolio. They had so many questions, most of which were unimportant but we had to answer them. You were right about pricing; this was their main worry and they took away some figures to look at and will come back to me next week. Overall, the meeting went well, the feedback from the customer was positive and we should get a decision next week.

This is what the reader wanted:

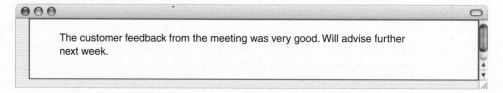

The customer feedback from the meeting was very good. Will advise further next week.

With regular email contacts it is important to explicitly discuss expectations about the transfer of information in terms of:

– **how much** information is required
– to what **level of detail**
– with which kind of **style** and **structure**
– at which **time**
– to which **people**.

Regarding that last point, be careful when copying an email to managers above you or above the level of the receiver. In some business cultures, this may simply be a method of keeping managers informed, and be expected from those senior in the organisation. However, in other cultures this simple act of copying a senior person in can be seen as aggressive escalation which explicitly criticises the receiver.

Tip 4 When you send urgent requests for information, be sensitive to the fact that people may be under a lot of pressure themselves. Use these ideas to request information more sensitively.

– Use polite phrases such as *Please could you ...?*
– Apologise in the email for placing added pressure on the person, for example *I'm sorry to ask ...* .
– Explain the context for your request which makes clear the difficult position you are in, for example *The reason for this is ...* .
– Express your thanks in a follow-up email when the information is delivered.

How could you rewrite the following email using the four ideas above? Compare your version with the sample email on page 162.

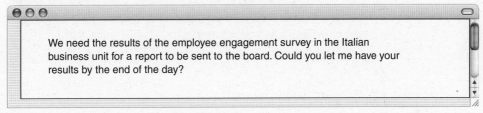

We need the results of the employee engagement survey in the Italian business unit for a report to be sent to the board. Could you let me have your results by the end of the day?

Tip 5 Finally, don't forget social protocols. Mistakes with basic forms of address (whether to use first name or surname, surname to be written first or second, choosing which of several family names to use) can irritate the receiver or make your email come across as rude. Make sure you find out what the rules are for the names, titles, greetings and endings of emails.

HOT TIPS

• Think carefully if it could be better to communicate by telephone than by email
• Write in a style and with the necessary information which supports the reader
• Request information politely – remember, you're creating work for the other person
• Research social rules for correspondence when dealing with unfamiliar cultures

27 International telephoning – talking to people

Many people these days prefer to email rather than call someone. However, as we shall examine here, telephoning has many advantages over email.

Why telephone?

Telephoning is an opportunity for building rapport

Managing relationships, as has been said many times in this book, is a key factor for success in working across cultures. Talking to someone on the phone means human contact, a chance to demonstrate interest in the person and to build common commitment to the relationship and work goals. But be careful: people see things differently across cultures. When you're calling someone who is highly results-focused, spending time on relationship-building could make you sound unprofessional and inefficient.

🌐 TRACK 32   Listen to the beginning of two calls Sam makes to two different customers. How does she try to build rapport in the first call? In the second call, what does she say to move the conversation quickly to a business topic? You can read the audio script and check your answers on page 162.

Telephoning is an opportunity for clear communication

A lot of topics are simply too complex to discuss via email. Talking to someone on the phone is an opportunity for dialogue. You can ask questions, clarify the other person's questions and clear up misunderstandings.

🌐 TRACK 33   Listen to another telephone call from Sam. What questions does she ask to clarify the meaning of the email she received from her colleague, Mary? You can read the audio script and check your answers on page 162.

Telephoning is an opportunity to get useful extra information

Working internationally and at a distance creates a lot of uncertainty in the minds of colleagues and puts pressure on effective communication. Telephoning provides an opportunity not only to deal with specific tasks, but also to find out general information on recent or future developments which could impact on your work.

🌐 TRACK 34   Listen to Sam's telephone call to her supplier, Jan. What question helps her to discover important information about developments in the Jan's company? You can read the audio script and check your answers on pages 162–3.

Telephoning is an opportunity to prevent conflict

Written communication has the potential to generate conflict where none exists, because quickly-written emails often come across as over-direct and critical. On the phone, there is greater opportunity to explain clearly your positive intentions, to hear misunderstanding as it happens and to clarify it quickly in order to stop any possible bad feeling.

TRACK 35   Listen to Sam talking to a colleague, John, about an email she sent him. How does she deal with the misunderstanding and avoid conflict? You can read the audio script and check your answers on page 163.

How often do you use similar techniques in *your* telephone calls at work?

How to make the most of your telephone calls

1 Starting

At the beginning of a call, whether it's scheduled or unscheduled, check that the person has time to talk to you, for example *Is this (still) a good time to talk?* People are busy and have many conflicting priorities.

2 Structuring

Quickly set out the main objectives of the call. If you know your partner prefers a less structured approach, use short phrases such as *Just to clarify objectives of the call briefly, ...* For someone who prefers to operate with a high degree of structure, other language may work better, for example *To start, I'd like to go over the agenda of our telephone call.*

3 Listening

We know that listening styles may differ across cultures, but active listening, where you use phrases like *I see*, *Really* or *That's interesting*, is very useful when you can't see the person you're talking to.

4 Confirming

As in a face-to-face meeting, confirm and agree to put in writing what was agreed on the phone, for example *Fine. Let's agree to do that. And I'll confirm that in writing.* This serves two purposes: it makes things clear, and it builds commitment when actions are documented in writing.

5 Closing

Knowing when to end a telephone call can be difficult. In some cultures the final part of the conversation small talk. In others, the call can end abruptly as people move to the next task. In a relationship-oriented context we might say *Nice talking to you and see you soon*. In a more task-oriented culture we might not waste time, and just say *Goodbye*.

Which of the above ideas do you plan to introduce in *your* next telephone call?

HOT TIPS

- Decrease the number of emails you send and increase the number of telephone calls you make
- Plan your calls with strategies for the opening, structuring, listening, confirming and closing phases
- Use the telephone and not email as the medium for relationship-building and conflict management

28 International teleconferencing – guidelines

Telephone conferences (or conference calls) are now a regular feature of working life, particularly for those involved in international project teams who need to stay in touch regularly without face-to-face meetings. In this unit we look at five challenges of the virtual meeting environment and provide simple solutions to make things work better.

Challenge 1 – The beginning of the conference call

It's really the responsibility of the chair to be first at the meeting in order that people can be properly welcomed as they arrive. During this phase it can be useful if the chair takes the lead in starting small talk or informal introductions *between* participants. For participants, their main task is simply to make sure their arrival is noted by the chair and to say hello. These opening moments can be a little chaotic, so saying less rather than more can keep things under control.

🌐 **TRACK 36**   Listen to the opening moments of a telephone conference call. What questions does the chair use to encourage the participants to interact? You can read the audio script and check your answers on page 163.

Challenge 2 – Starting well

As there is no opportunity in this virtual environment for strangers to physically shake hands, it's important for the chair to introduce new people more explicitly.

I should start by introducing John from the London office. He's an IT expert and will be supporting with the SAP sub-project. John, would you like to say a few words?

It can also be a good idea to discuss some basic speaking and listening guidelines at the start. This is important in a telephone conference environment where nobody can simply look around the table and see who understands or who wants to speak next. Here are some ideas for guidelines.

- Participants should state their own name before giving an opinion – this clarifies who's speaking – and the name of the relevant person when asking for an opinion – this clarifies who should speak next. *This is Bob Headley and this question is for Mike Seymour. What do you think about ...?*

- Participants should express agreement verbally – *I agree* – rather than with silence.

- The chair can interrupt to keep the meeting on track, for example *Xavier, sorry to interrupt. Can I remind you of the agreed rules? Please ask a question to a named person and not just openly to the group.*

🎧 **TRACK 37**   Listen to an extract in which the chair is giving guidelines. Which of the guidelines above is *not* proposed by the chair, and why? You can read the audio script and check your answers on page 163.

Which guidelines would be useful for *your* international conference calls?

In smaller groups and where people know each other well, a chair can be less directive and more flexible in style in order to encourage group interaction. Try these ideas.

- Ask open questions to the whole group to stimulate creative thinking, for example *What does everyone think about this idea?*

- Allow time for all participants to speak.

- Encourage participants to comment on each other's ideas to create a group solution, for example *Jan, what do you think about Enrico's suggestion?*

Challenge 3 – Listening effectively – a participant's perspective

Listening as a participant in a telephone conference can be more demanding than in a face-to-face meeting. The lack of visual information from the body language of the speakers and the lower sound quality from conference call technology means it's often hard to understand both the basic message and the intention behind the message. Creating an opportunity to speak and enter a discussion – whether to clarify or give an opinion – is also more challenging, as you can't indicate with your hand or by your facial expression that you want to speak.

🔊 TRACK 38   Listen to two examples of participants using different tactics to enter a discussion. Which tactics do João and Maria use? You can read the audio script and check your answers on pages 163–4.

Which tactic would work better in *your* international meetings?

Challenge 4 – Speaking effectively – a participant's perspective

Getting people to listen to you can be difficult in virtual meetings, especially with large numbers of participants who prefer to give opinions rather than spend time understanding the ideas of others. Use these techniques to create a better impact as a speaker.

- Separate complex information into structured chunks, simplifying wherever possible and allowing questions at key moments.

- Centre the presentation concretely around supporting documentation – a PowerPoint presentation or an Excel spreadsheet – which people can view and follow you through.

- Integrate the audience's views / concerns and points of view to keep your message as accessible and relevant as possible.

- Make your voice interesting to listen to – positive tone, varied intonation, right volume and tempo.

- Finish with a question which forces the other participants to respond to your ideas.

🔊 TRACK 39   Listen to Derek explaining his views on a recent production problem. Which question does he use to finish his input? Why does he use this type of question? You can read the audio script and check your answers on page 164.

How far could you use questions like this in your international conference calls?

Challenge 5 – Closing

When leading a conference call, allow more time than usual for explicit summarising and consensus-checking at the end. Participants, particularly those with lower language competence, will need this opportunity to hear the main points again and to confirm that they agree.

Before we close, let me just go over the main points of the meeting again to check understanding and to confirm agreement from everyone. So, on the first point, we've decided to …

And don't forget to follow up the conference call with an email summarising the discussion and decisions taken, and asking for ideas on how to improve communication in the next call.

HOT TIPS

- As chair, take responsibility for effective interaction: handling arrivals, setting guidelines at the start of the meeting, giving an explicit summary at the close
- As a participant, choose listening and speaking behaviours which will avoid any confusion caused by the fact that people can't see you, and you can't see them

29 International negotiations – mapping diversity

Everybody knows the word *negotiation*. The challenge is that people come to the negotiating table with very different expectations of exactly what and how to negotiate. Here we analyse these differences.

Dimensions of diversity

In the table are eight dimensions of negotiating diversity which you can use to compare and contrast negotiating styles across cultures. Underline the parts of the text which describe your own approach to negotiating.

1 Basic concept of negotiation

In some cultures a negotiation is conducted in a spirit of relationship-building and partnership. The aim in the early stages is simply to get to know each other. This slower, softer relationship approach can be very different from more competitive and goal-oriented cultural styles which focus aggressively on getting to an agreement and winning the best deal.

2 Negotiator profile

In some cultures negotiators are selected according to ability – their expertise, experience or past achievements. In others, negotiators may be present simply because of their status and seniority in the company, rather than their negotiating skills or business knowledge.

3 Negotiator role

In some cultures an individual is given responsibility to negotiate. In others, negotiation is conducted by a group or team. The role of decision-maker may also differ. In some cultures the real decision-maker may not be at the table, or, if they are at the table, they may not be speaking, but observing silently.

4 Issues and priorities for negotiation

In some cultures people prefer to begin with general principles. In others, the negotiation moves quickly to detail. Some negotiators want to talk about solutions; others focus more on risks. Some want to talk about price; others agree price quickly, but want to discuss quality and delivery issues at length. In cultures with a focus on harmony, people begin with points of agreement. Negotiators from more competitive environments, or more tolerant of conflict, may go straight to points of disagreement.

5 Rituals and protocols

All cultures have rituals and protocols about the social component of a negotiation, for example how people are welcomed at the start of the negotiation (are gifts given, or an opening speech by a senior manager?); seating protocols (where do the most senior people sit?); entertaining (what level of social entertainment is expected?).

6 Communication style

Some cultures accept directness, emotionality and even aggressiveness. Others prefer indirectness, emotional neutrality and harmony. Some cultures will expect a negotiation to be a highly structured meeting. For others, it can be more of a flexible discussion.

7 Time

Different attitudes to time can impact on negotiation in a number of ways. Some cultures with a longer-term mindset may tolerate a negotiation process which takes weeks or months, frustrating those can-do cultures where things happen more quickly. Within a negotiation, it's common to see a clash between those want to follow strictly the timetable or agenda set for the day, and those who prefer to work with less structure and time focus.

8 Agreement and legal contract

In some cultures verbal agreement is a binding commitment. In others, what was agreed at one meeting may be open to negotiation again later if circumstances change. The type and status of any final legal contract will be different across cultures, often simply because there are different legal requirements relating to contracts in each nation state. Some cultures may require a level of detail – especially regarding the identification or risk and responsibility in case of breach of contract – which will frustrate others.

Read through the table again and identify differences to your approach which you have experienced when negotiating across cultures.

Experiences of diversity

🌐 TRACK 40   Listen to three international negotiating anecdotes. Which of the differences in negotiating style analysed in the table explains the speaker's experience in each anecdote? You can read the audio script and check your answers on page 164.

In the third anecdote the speaker describes a strategy for international negotiators when he says that it is important to 'know the culture and use the right cultural tools which will get you to an agreement.' How far do you agree with him? Which 'cultural tools' do you use in *your* working context?

In the next module we'll look in detail at strategies for managing negotiation style differences identified in this unit.

HOT TIPS

- Research the negotiating style of your counterpart by reading country-specific briefings
- Ask experienced colleagues inside the company and any external contacts you have for their experience of the target culture
- Use the table presented in this module to map possible gaps in approach and style between yourself and the people you negotiate with

30 International negotiations – clarifying the process

In his book *Negotiation – readings, exercises and cases* Daniel Lewicki argues that it's important to know how well each negotiator understands the other's culture.

Effective negotiators can then decide which kind of negotiating process to use. He identifies five main processes:

1 Use a middleman

If neither you nor your counterpart share an understanding of each other's mindset and approach, then it may be better to use a middleman, someone who has knowledge of both cultures, to create better understanding and prevent conflict.

2 Persuade them do it your way

If you have little understanding of your counterpart's culture but they understand yours, it may be simpler to ask or persuade your counterpart to follow your way of doing things.

3 Do it their way

On the other hand, if you are very familiar with your counterpart's culture and they are unfamiliar with your way of doing things, it could make sense to work with their procedures and approach to maximise the collaboration opportunities.

4 Negotiate the process

If both parties have reasonable knowledge of the other's mindset and approach, the strategy could be to negotiate about the negotiation process itself, to clarify expectations in relation to roles, to deadlines, to detail of information, and so on.

5 Improvise

Where both parties have excellent knowledge of the other's business culture it may be possible to improvise according to each situation, as there is little potential for misunderstanding.

Test your intercultural sensitivity

🎧 **TRACK 41**   Listen to three extracts from the opening of negotiations between John Hansen, an IT software supplier, and different global customers. Which strategy does John use in each negotiation? You can read the audio script and check your answers on page 165.

Extract 1   ....

Extract 2   ....

Extract 3   ....

Negotiating how to negotiate

One of the strategies identified by Lewicki was to coordinate the negotiation process itself – to discuss and agree how to manage diversity, in order to create a clear platform for discussion and collaboration. The following four-step approach can be used to achieve this.

Step 1   Propose to clarify dimensions of the negotiation process
I'd like to clarify one or two things about the discussion process before we start …

Step 2   Identify and explain the diversity dimension(s) to clarify
I think we have different ideas about what quality means …

Step 3 Propose and negotiate a way to manage the diversity dimension(s)
Perhaps we should start by defining in more detail what we mean by quality ...

Step 4 Agree a way forward
What do you think? Would this be useful?

🔊 **TRACK 42** Listen and read this extract from an international negotiation and underline the language which Claudio uses for each of the above steps. You can check your answers on page 165.

Claudio	Before we start, I think it would be useful to clarify a little how we plan to negotiate today. One of the main issues is how we see our roles. From our side, we have a lot of scope to discuss all the issues, but in terms of any final agreement we have to go back to our senior management for approval. That means for us we should see this part of the negotiation as a first discussion phase and we would be looking to finalise things at another meeting at some point in the future. How does that sound?
Martha	Well, it's good that you raised this, as our understanding was quite different. We expected to close the deal today. Our role here is really one of decision maker but we appreciate your situation is a little different. I would propose a form of compromise in that any decision we reach today should be seen as a 90% solution with 10% to finalise at a future meeting. Otherwise, it may be better to wait.
Claudio	No, that's fine from our point of view. I think we have scope to agree to a 90% solution which we can move to a deal by the end of the month?
Martha	Good. So we can begin with ...

The above process works as an example of how to open a negotiation – to actually negotiate the process of negotiation itself. There are no guarantees that counterparts will accept this approach, but it can be a strategy to demonstrate openness and to win commitment to achieving mutual success.

HOT TIPS

- Adopt a flexible approach when entering the international negotiation arena
- Select one of the five strategies for international negotiation based on your assessment of each negotiating partner's knowledge of the other's culture
- Where possible, negotiate the negotiation process at the start to create a transparent platform for discussion

Building relationships

'If you can be interested in other people, you can own the world.'

Jay Abraham

Doing business effectively depends on your ability to build and cultivate meaningful relationships with a range of contacts, including colleagues, managers, suppliers, customers, and even coaches and external consultants.

It's very important to think carefully about who specifically you need to build relationships with, and how to do it differently according to each cultural and interpersonal context.

People have very different expectations of business relationships. On the one hand, some believe it is important to establish a close personal relationship before getting down to business. Others see results as a first priority, with relationship-building second.

The next five units will give you ideas on how to improve your relationship-building skills with techniques suitable for a range of intercultural business contexts.

31 **The importance of relationships**

32 **Managing first contacts**

33 **Building rapport**

34 **Asking questions to build better relationships**

35 **Influencing people in your network**

31 The importance of relationships

One of the challenges of working across cultures is dealing with people who are different from ourselves. It can take a lot of effort to engage with people who are different to us and to take the first steps in a conversation with people from another culture.

Building relationships across cultures requires a mindset – a way of thinking – which is open, proactive and strategic. You also need to be able to analyse the cultural context and to behave flexibly according to the situation.

International mindsets

Read how three professionals described their international mindsets. Which of these do you share? How would you describe your own mindset?

'I'm just curious. I take the approach that I can always learn from others, so relationship-building is partly an investment in my own development. But it's also interesting how curiosity helps to build relationships. If you're curious and ask questions, people really warm to you. Of course, you have to be careful in some contexts. Asking too many personal questions or the wrong personal questions can be misunderstood.'

I share / don't share this mindset because ....

'For me tolerance is important. When I used to meet new people I tended to judge them – often negatively – according to my own values and behaviours. But experience has told me to stay interested in people even when I think that I have nothing in common with them at first. And then over time you discover things in common and you have a foundation to build a working relationship.'

I share / don't share this mindset because ....

'For me the main thing is to be first. What I mean is I like to be the one starting the conversations, filling in the difficult silences with a comment or a question just to keep the conversation going. I've found that if one person does this, in a one-to-one conversation or in a group, relationships work much better.'

I share / don't share this mindset because ....

My international mindset is ....

....

....

....

Intercultural relationship-building skills

The Centre for Intercultural Learning at the Canadian Foreign Service Institute has described a set of relationship-building skills shown by interculturally effective people. Look at the checklist based on their research and decide how far you have developed these relationship skills. Score yourself 1 (low) to 5 (high).

An interculturally effective person ...	Score 1–5
1 has a socialising strategy:	
– makes an effort to socialise with individuals from other cultures (will arrange meetings with individuals and find time to meet the wider community, e.g. go to festivals, music events, etc., even during short visits).	_____
– does not spend too much time with colleagues from own cultures or fellow expatriates – does not become isolated from other cultures.	_____
2 has a language strategy:	
– invests time in learning the local language when abroad and can manage simple phrases and some basic conversation.	_____
– will regularly ask for translations or the meanings of words in the local language.	_____
3 knows other cultures:	
– able to describe key social protocols and codes of other cultures.	_____
– is able to assess the importance of relationships and style of relationship-building in other cultures.	_____
4 is sensitive to stereotypes:	
– understands how people from his/her own culture may be perceived in other cultures.	_____
– is able to avoid stereotypical thinking about individuals from other cultures which could lead to negative judgements.	_____
5 knows how he/she is seen in other cultures:	
– will ask for feedback on his/her behaviour to check it is appropriate for other cultures.	_____
– will get positive feedback from international colleagues that he/she is friendly and fits well into other cultures.	_____

If you score less than 3 in any one dimension (or less than 30 overall), make an action plan to build on your strengths and minimise any weaknesses (or risks) to your international relationship-building style.

HOT TIPS

- Be curious about others. If others think you're interested in them, they're more likely to show interest in you!
- Avoid spending too much time with people you already know at international events. Take every opportunity to broaden your network
- Learn to ask the right questions which make social conversation work

32 Managing first contacts

First meetings are obviously very important for establishing a good working relationship. A lot can depend on first impressions. Handling these moments well is an intercultural competence which demands a great deal of energy, concentration, tolerance and flexibility.

Across cultures, first meetings are managed very differently. For example, in some situations an exchange of gifts may be an important part of the first meeting. It's a good idea to research what is expected if you're visiting a new country, or receiving important visitors from a culture you don't know.

In addition to doing research, it's also important to develop attitudes and behaviours for dealing with first meetings.

WorldWork, a London-based consultancy, has developed an intercultural development tool called *The International Profiler*, which shows two very different styles of dealing with people you don't know.

Take a look at the two styles below and decide which is closer to your own approach.

	Potential advantages	Potential risks
Style 1 people ...		
enjoy meeting others from different backgrounds with different values	can build personal network quickly	may be seen as 'too friendly'
actively initiate personal contact with new people	can help others to become comfortable	may lose focus on objectives
find it easy to approach and talk to strangers	can learn about other cultures quickly	may fail to develop key relationships
Style 2 people ...		
prefer to be with familiar and like-minded people	can remain task-focused at all times	may take longer to learn the culture
are seldom the first to initiate personal contacts with new people	are less likely to be manipulated by unfamiliar faces	may come across as 'unfriendly'
prefer strong and deep friendships with a few close friends to big networks of acquaintances	can build meaningful and long-lasting relationships	may fail to build necessary networks

What would you identify as the main advantage and risk of your own style? Make a note below of what you can do to maximise your strengths and minimise the risks of your approach.

To maximise my main **strength** I could ....

To minimise the main **risk** I could ....

Having a learning mindset is a key to intercultural success.

Getting the basics right

Here is a four-phase model with ideas for handling a visitor to your office. As you read through, note down typical things you might say or ask in each of the phases.

Phase 1 – Introductions

First meetings can be moments with a lot of uncertainty and anxiety. Why not take the lead and introduce yourself first to start the process of getting to know each other?

When you introduce yourself, think carefully about:

– which name (first and / or surname) to use
– whether your counterpart may expect to hear a professional or academic title, for example Dr, Head of Marketing, and so on
– how important any exchange of business cards is.

It can also be a good idea to start with a question which checks the other person's name: *Mr Hentschell, would you like to … ?* This shows that you're already thinking about the other person.

Secondly, if the other person might have difficulty remembering or pronouncing your name, offer them a simple form: *Please call me … .*

Finally, be proactive at introducing less proactive contacts to each other in order to develop better communication in groups, for example *Can I introduce you to … ?* or *Have you two met?*

What else could you typically say or ask in this phase?

Phase 2 – Polite offers

As the host of a visitor to your office, it will be your job to keep things moving with some polite offers, for example *May I take your coat?* or *Can I get you something to drink?* It's important to do this in order to communicate courtesy and warmth to the visitor. If you're the visitor, make sure you respond positively to these offers, for example *That's very kind of you.* or *I'd love a cup of coffee.*

What would you typically say or ask in this phase?

Phase 3 – Small talk

This is a difficult thing to get right, but it's a very important part of a first meeting. If you're the host, ask about accommodation, travel arrangements, business and even the weather to get the conversation going. Listen carefully for things in your guest's responses which allow you to ask follow-up questions, for example *You mentioned India. Was that a business trip or for a holiday?* Remember, asking questions is the basis of small talk, so it's important to develop your question skills.

What else could you typically say or ask in this phase?

Phase 4 – Getting down to business

As we have said, in some cultures people like to get down to business quickly, whereas others like to spend more time building trust and establishing a close personal relationship.

As host or guest, you have to observe and listen carefully for the moment when you should start discussing business. This is usually indicated with verbal signals like *Right* or *OK* or by non-verbal gestures such as moving to the meeting table, taking out papers or putting on glasses. You can change the focus to business very explicitly by saying *OK, shall we get started?*

What else could you typically say or ask in this phase?

🔊 TRACK 43   Listen to two meetings in which Kwame Luthuli from Ghana greets different visitors to his office for the first time. Which questions does he ask in the small talk phase in the two conversations? You can read the audio script and check your answers on pages 165–6. Which conversation do you think is more successful, and why?

HOT TIPS

- Research how first meetings are conducted in the target culture as a basic part of your preparation
- Build greater awareness of your own typical behaviours in first meetings and then try to develop more flexibility to deal with a wider range of situations
- Use the four-phase model above to plan what to say and what to do the next time you have to manage a first meeting with new contacts

33 Building rapport

Rapport – the establishment of a sympathetic and harmonious relationship – is the ultimate objective of building a relationship. Just as relationships are defined and valued differently across cultures, so there exists a range of rapport-building styles.

Three steps to rapport

Understanding different expectations of rapport is an important first step in developing rapport-building competence across cultures.

The second step is to know your own style – unless you know yourself, you will never manage others.

The third and final step is to analyse the style of the individuals you meet and be able to manage conversations with them effectively.

Step 1 – Understanding rapport-building styles across cultures

Susanne Zaninelli, in her famous comparison of German and American attitudes to business relationships, contrasts two very different styles – that of the coconut (German) and the peach (American).

This model identifies differences between very task-oriented individuals (coconuts) and more relationship-sensitive people (peaches).

The coconut

The coconut individual has only a thin and hard shell of personal space to share in the business arena – this person is more focused on the task than making friends.

Politeness means respecting privacy and allowing personal relations to develop over time. It takes a long time to really break through the hard outer shell into the truly personal area, to become *friends* and begin a genuinely personal relationship.

Profile:

General approach: neutral, authentic, reserved, values personal space
Communication style: doesn't 'play' a role, is honest, uses silence, is direct
Time: lets the relationship develop naturally over time

The peach

The peach individual is very different, and expects friendship to develop quickly in a warm and very personal way.

You go quickly into the warm flesh of the peach when you meet by asking lots of personal questions to really get to know each other.

The priority here is warmth and enthusiasm for the other person, which demonstrates politeness. However, the truly private self – the stone in the centre – perhaps remains hidden from view.

Profile:

General approach:	makes efforts to speak to others, values small talk
Communication style:	enthusiastic, proactive, polite, uses lots of questions
Time:	makes a positive relationship happen quickly

Coconuts and peaches often have problems building rapport with each other. For example, coconuts frequently report that peaches are superficial people who appear friendly when in fact the real motive is to win at business. On the other hand, the peach can find the coconut individual cold and impolite.

Step 2 – Understanding your own rapport-building style

Analyse your own rapport-building style using the coconut-peach dimensions below. Give yourself a percentage for each dimension.

PERSONAL PROFILE

General approach

0%   100%

reserved / distant   close / value small talk

Communication style

0%   100%

honest / direct / authentic   enthusiastic / proactive / questions

Time

0%   100%

relationship happens over time   relationship happens quickly

---

Now comes the important part – to find out how correctly you have evaluated your own style, you need to ask a close business contact if he or she agrees with your scores!

Step 3 – Managing the rapport-building styles of others

The final step is to map the rapport-building style of your key contacts and to develop communication strategies for building rapport effectively with these different people.

🔊 **TRACK 44**   Listen to extracts from two lunch conversations between Javier and two new international colleagues, Jean and Alex. Which of the two colleagues is the peach and which is the coconut? How does Javier try to build rapport with the two visitors differently? You can read the audio script and check your answers on page 166.

How well can you build effective relationships using different rapport-building styles? Make some notes and then read Unit 34 for more ideas.

HOT TIPS

- Develop your understanding of how rapport is defined and developed differently across cultures
- Build greater awareness of your own rapport-building style and the way it may create positive and negative experiences for other people
- Map the rapport-building styles of your key contacts and make sure you are building relationships in the right way with each person

34   Asking questions to build better relationships

In many cultural contexts asking questions is an effective way of building rapport. People like to feel another person is showing real interest in their situation and their views. However, as we've noted many times already, you have to be careful about the subject of those questions.

Questions for building intercultural rapport

Phase 1

Begin by asking questions to discover the right subject to talk about.

So, do you have any experience of …?
Have you ever been to …? | Is this your first time …?

Of course, it may not be so easy to find the right subject. You may need to do some research to find out appropriate things to talk about. Try to focus on a topic interesting to your partner, rather than one of interest to yourself.

Take care to balance relationship and task-focused questions according to the style and expectations of the other person. If someone is more a peach (see Unit 33), make sure your style is not too task-oriented. If someone is more a coconut, don't get too personal, as it will make them feel uncomfortable.

Questions for the peach:

I guess you're tired after the flight. So take some time to relax.
I hope you're free for dinner tonight?
Is everything OK with the hotel?

Questions for the coconut:

How is the reorganisation going? I heard it's a tough process.
Are you busy with the Telcom project? I heard it's going well.
Is Peter working with you again in the project?

Phase 2

Once you have identified a subject which you feel your partner is interested in, then develop it with a series of open follow-up questions:

When will you …? | Why did you …? | How do you …? | What are you …?

In this phase it's a good idea to balance questions which really ask for information with questions which simply give the other person the chance to talk comfortably about their own areas of expertise and experience.

Phase 3

Begin the process of connecting to people by signalling that you have points in common – perhaps a shared experience, network or background – with questions which explore what is shared. This can create the feeling of a mutual understanding which is so critical for building rapport.

Same network: *I think we both know Guy Tate. Have you seen him recently?*
Same background: *Your background is IT? Mine too. What kind of IT work?*
Same experience: *I also lived in Shanghai. How did you find it?*

🎧 **TRACK 45**   Listen to a conversation over lunch between Ben and his supplier, Alejandro, both based in Paris. Answer the following questions. You can read the audio script and check your answers on page 166.

Phase 1   Which question does Ben ask to start the discussion about Mexico?

Phase 2   How many open questions does Ben ask about Mexico?

Phase 3   What do Ben and Alejandro discover that they have in common?

In which of *your* working contexts would it be useful to structure conversations with this three-phase approach?

- Ask questions which communicate real interest in the other person
- Focus on helping someone to talk about what interests *them* rather than what interests you
- Work hard to find points in common with the other person
- Direct questions towards shared experiences as a way to develop mutual understanding

35 Influencing people in your network

When you work internationally managing relationships isn't simply about building positive relations with people. It also means being able to influence others. You will need to develop a *range* of influencing styles for different contexts.

Influencing across cultures

Review these influencing styles and think about which you could use in your work.

Communicate benefits – 'push' / 'pull' styles

There are two styles for communicating benefits. You can convince people that you know what they need – the 'push' style. Or you can ask people what they want first, and then deliver some form of tailored solution to satisfy this want – the 'pull' style.

'Push' style – recommendation	'Pull' style – questions
What you need to do is ...	*What do you need?*
I think you should ...	*What do you think you should ...?*
I really think it's important to ...	*Could we ...?*

🎧 **TRACK 46** Listen to extracts from two conversations in which Luis tries to influence international colleagues. In which does he use the 'push' style and in which the 'pull' style? Which specific questions does he use in the 'pull' conversation? You can read the audio script and check your answers on page 167.

Cultivate trust

People are more likely to be influenced by those they trust. To trust you, people need to believe you are competent – you have the right expertise for the job to be done; and that you have integrity – you are fair, consistent and a person with clear moral values.

You can build trust in the following ways.

1 Show interest in people's needs, opinions and feelings
   I understand that ...
   I appreciate that ...

2 Highlight ideas which you share with other people
   I think we both want to ...
   We agree that ...

3 Focus on collaboration as the way forward
   We need to work together to ...
   We should discuss how we can ...

How do *you* cultivate trust at work?

Be transparent

People who don't communicate clearly will be misunderstood, and they will fail to influence. But clear communication is more than simply using the right words. As we have seen, people who also explicitly state their intentions (and positive motivation) behind key messages are more likely to get their message across and influence others.

1 Communicate clearly your intention to do something
   My intention is to ...
   What I really want to do is ...

2 Communicate clearly your intention *not* to do something
   My intention is not to ...
   What I don't want to do is ...

🔊 **TRACK 47** Listen to Helena presenting the need for a talent management initiative to line managers. What does she say very explicitly is her intention, and what is *not* her intention? You can read the audio script and check your answers on page 167.

Make people like you

People are more open to influence from people they like and feel they have something in common with.

Be strong

We can be influenced by those who communicate their ideas forcefully. People who are direct and to the point and who state alternatives in clear terms can influence others. Strong communicators often use the following strategies.

1 State personal conviction explicitly
   I'm convinced that ...
   I really believe ...

2 Use strong language
   It's would be very unwise not to ...
   We have to ...

3 Argue forcefully against opposite views
   We can't ... because ...
   His idea wouldn't work because ...

4 Refer clearly to negative consequences of inaction
   If we don't, then we ...
   Either we implement my solution or we face ...

🔊 TRACK 48   Listen to Jacob discussing the location of the next international team meeting with his colleague. Which of the above strategies does he use to communicate his opinions strongly? You can read the audio script and check your answers on page 167.

How far could you use this kind influencing style in your work?

Look to the future

Individuals who provide a clear vision of the future with step-by-step guidance on how to achieve what they want are seen as more engaging and influential.

Be confident

If you communicate self-confidence, it's possible that you can influence without sophisticated arguments and solid data.

Show optimism

Negativity is seldom inspirational. Positive thinkers with energy and enthusiasm for creative solutions are more appealing and influential.

Be prepared

Your ability to influence will always depend on your ability to deal with objections to your proposition. Always anticipate objections in advance and plan counter-arguments accordingly.

🌐 **TRACK 49**   Listen to an extract from an international departmental meeting discussing investment in new computers. What does Anton say is the IT problem? You can read the audio script and check your answers on pages 167–8.

What do you think of Haukur's influencing style, with direct and immediate disagreement using prepared arguments? How far could it work in *your* international contexts?

Which of these influencing styles are most useful for you in *your* working contexts?

HOT TIPS

- Develop a range of influencing styles
- Adapt your influencing style to the person and the cultural context
- Use an influencing style which you feel comfortable with

Working in international teams

'This is terribly important – to choose the right people to work with you. I don't just mean those who can do the job, but people that you like, people that you can feel you can trust, people that you enjoy being with.'   Charles Handy

Successful international teams share a number of characteristics: competent and motivated team members, effective leadership, clear roles and good communication.

In order to become a high-performing team, Bruce Tuckman suggested that there are separate stages through which a team has to pass. These are comparable in many ways to stages of individual growth: infancy, childhood, adolescence and adulthood.

Here are his four stages of team development:

Forming   team gets together and begins to explore its task and its own dynamic

Storming   differences and conflicts emerge and have to be managed to move forward

Norming   tasks are clarified / team works cooperatively with common understanding

Performing   trust is established / team is working creatively and using its diversity

Tuckman later added a fifth stage, **adjourning**: managing the break-up of the team once the job is done.

In this module we will use the Tuckman model as a framework to look at ways in which teams perform.

36 **Building common understanding**

37 **Understanding and preventing conflict**

38 **Dealing with conflict**

39 **Creating a clear framework for teamwork**

40 **Getting the best out of your team**

36 Building common understanding

When teams come together, it's very important that team members get to know each other as quickly as possible, and begin the team-building process which Tuckman described as *forming*.

For new teams there is usually a kick-off meeting that provides time for everyone to get to know each other. This kick-off meeting also provides an opportunity to clarify the main objectives of the team and its schedule for the coming months.

At kick-off meetings it's vital that people exchange both professional and personal information. This is particularly true for those who will be working in 'virtual' teams – meeting via telephone and teleconferencing – where there are far fewer opportunities to establish common understanding.

Here are three ideas to help develop common understanding in the team.

Present a clear professional profile

For people to work effectively with you, they need to understand your role, your special capabilities and the particular mindset which you bring to the team. It's typical at team meetings to make a short personal introductory presentation to other team members. Such presentations should cover the following topics:

- responsibilities within the team
- knowledge and skills you have which are relevant for the team's tasks
- experience of working in teams
- background personal information
- positive expectations about working in the team.

In this unit you'll hear extracts from meetings between members of an international project team working for Bonn Homme, an insurance company which plans to develop a single Global Leadership Academy. The team consists of HR, IT and Finance specialists. John Hansen from Denmark is the project leader.

🎧 TRACK 50   Listen to the personal introductions of John Hansen and Jim Chambers, his deputy, at the team kick-off meeting. Which of the five items above does each speaker mention? You can read the audio script and check your answers on page 168.

Which of the two introductions do you prefer? How would you introduce yourself at an international project team kick-off meeting?

Get to know others in the team

It's important that you tell team members about yourself not only in formal meetings, but also during breaks and when socialising after work. During these informal moments you should also take every opportunity to ask questions in order to get to know the other team members.

Responsibilities within the team

So, what are your responsibilities exactly?

Knowledge and skills they have which are relevant for the team's tasks

You did some leadership training in the past. What kind of training did you do?

Experience of working in international teams

You said you worked in Australia. What were you doing there?

Background personal information

So tell me a little bit more about ...

Positive expectations about working in the team

So why are you looking forward to this project?

🔊 **TRACK 51**   Listen to other members of the team, Samantha Dolores and Anshuman Pandey, getting to know each other over a coffee. Which two areas does Samantha focus on? You can read the audio script and check your answers on page 168.

Samantha asks a question about 'problems' at the end of the conversation. How far do you think this is the right kind of question during a kick-off meeting?

Understand and clarify the team's goals

International teamwork can involve a great deal of uncertainty and resistance.

Uncertainty is often present because the precise targets of an international team's work may not be fully defined, and may evolve over time as information is collected and different possible solutions are tested across business units.

Resistance is often present because international teams often work to deliver standard solutions which create a lot of change with little clear benefit to the local organisations.

In these circumstances it's vital that international team members work hard to clarify and develop understanding of, and commitment to, the team's goals. Without understanding and commitment, an international team will quickly become inefficient.

🔊 **TRACK 52**   Listen to Jim Chambers talking again to his new team colleagues. Why is Samantha unclear about the goals of the team? How does Jim clarify the goals and try to build her commitment to the project? You can read the audio script and check your answers on page 169.

How often do you try to clarify goals and build the commitment of other members of *your* international team? Do you see this as the job of the leader, everyone's responsibility, or both?

HOT TIPS

- Communicate a clear professional profile so that people understand what you bring to the team
- Get to know others in your team quickly
- Ensure everyone understands and is committed to the team's goals

37   Understanding and preventing conflict

Tuckman's team-building model suggests that some conflict, which he calls *storming*, is an inevitable part of a team's development after *forming*.

People join the team with various expectations and it's only natural that there will be disagreements and different ideas about what the team is and should be doing at the beginning of a project. Indeed, there may be a benefit if different ideas about what the team should be doing are surfaced – that is, brought up and discussed – early on in the life of the project.

Team members need to *understand* the sources of team conflict. They also need to prevent disagreements and different ideas from damaging the team.

Understanding the sources of conflict

The main sources of conflict experienced in international teams are:

- culture – differences in the way people think and behave
- organisation – different processes and priorities in the business units of international companies
- resources – pressure created by increased workload and under-resourcing
- communication – dominant speakers, overuse of email, lack of listening
- personality – lack of tolerance, impatience, inflexibility.

TRACK 53   Listen to a telephone conversation between Nathalie and Andy, two members of an international project. What do you think is the main source of their conflict? You can read the audio script and check your answers on page 169.

What are the typical conflicts you have experienced in *your* international teams? What were the sources of the conflict?

Preventing conflict

Conflict can destroy team spirit and trust. In order to prevent this, it's important to be proactive at the beginning of the team project.

Build awareness of the potential for conflict at the team kick-off

- Acknowledge that challenges exist and stress the need for close cooperation.
  I know that parts of this project may be difficult, but we will succeed if we work together.
- Agree a way to deal with any disagreements openly, constructively and fairly.
  I think we should discuss problems openly inside the team immediately.
- Stress the value that different working styles represent for the team.
  The different working styles in this team can help us find creative solutions.

TRACK 54   Listen to a team leader, Alena, at a kick-off meeting. What conflict management process does she suggest? You can read the audio script and check your answers on page 169.

How far do you think this could work in *your* international teams?

Minimise the potential for damaging conflict during the life of the project

- Spend time with team members and surface possible sources of conflict.
  Paolo, you don't seem very happy with our decision. What's your opinion?
  So, Elena, how are you feeling about the project at the moment? Happy?
  Stefanie, how do you think Bob feels about the project?
- Clarify possible misunderstandings immediately.
  Sorry, do you mean that …?
  Sorry, maybe I didn't explain very well. What I meant to say was …
  Elena, I don't think Paolo meant to criticise you. I think he was saying that …

- Deal proactively with problem people in team meetings.
  People who dominate: *Kurt, can I stop you there? I'd like to hear some of the views of the others around the table.*
  People who blame others: *Bob, I'm not sure it's fair to say it was Stefanie's fault. Instead I think we should …*
  People who interrupt: *Guy, can you let Stefanie finish her point? Thanks. Stefanie, you were saying …*
  People who are too complex: *Bob, could you slow down a little? It's difficult for us to follow you. Could you explain again why …?*

🎧 **TRACK 55**   Listen to a short extract from a team meeting. Which kind of problem person does the chair of the meeting have to deal with? You can read the audio script and check your answers on page 169.

Which types of problem communicator do you have in *your* international team meetings? How do you manage them?

The best way to handle potentially damaging conflict is to prevent it from happening in the first place. In addition to the above ideas, you should encourage regular and constructive feedback within the team (see Unit 43), involve everyone in finding solutions to problems to build engagement, and take time out to have fun with dinners, events, and surprise activities to create a positive atmosphere.

HOT TIPS

- View conflicts as both inevitable and necessary to finding creative and effective solutions
- Prepare for conflict by analysing possible sources of conflict in your international teams
- Agree a way of handling conflicts with the team

38 Dealing with conflict

People deal with conflict in different ways. The focus here is on the 'win-win' approach.

The 'win-win' approach to conflict conversations

The six tips in this approach will help you to resolve conflicts in a way which allows everyone to feel positive about the outcome.

1 Open the conversation positively

It's very important to create a positive framework for the discussion right at the beginning.

Thank you for finding time for this meeting ...
I'm sure we can find a solution to this situation ...

2 Respect different perspectives

You have to respect different perspectives on the 'facts of a situation' and the needs behind these perspectives.

I understand that you see this as a lack of trust ...
So, for you the main issue is a lack of consultation ...

3 Recognise emotions and identities

You have to recognise and manage emotions.

I can hear that you are very angry about ...
I understand your frustration, but let's try to move away from blaming people to ...

4 Explore a range of solutions

Suggesting a solution yourself is one possibility, but it may be better to ask the people involved to find a creative solution themselves.

How far would you consider ...?
What do you think could solve the situation?

5 Minimise loss of face

Asking individuals to accept a compromise solution can be very difficult for some people. One strategy to open people to new solutions is to minimise the loss of face involved in accepting the idea.

I think this is a good solution. It just means you need to ...
Doing this represents a very small concession on your side.

6 Celebrate success at the end of the conversation

After reaching a solution celebrate success and create a positive frame for future cooperation in the team.

I think this was a really useful discussion and we can now move on to ...
This is a very good solution and this enables us to ...

🔊 **TRACK 56**   Listen to a meeting to discuss a conflict between a team leader, Paula, and a team member, Xiang, about a transfer to another project. What is the negotiated solution? Which of the six tips are used in the conversation? You can read the audio script and check your answers on pages 169–70.

How far could you use these tips to deal with conflict in *your* work?

HOT TIPS
- Understand how conflict is managed differently for personality and cultural reasons
- Try not to solve conflict using a strategy which other people cannot accept
- As much as possible, use the 'win-win' approach

39 Creating a clear framework for teamwork

When groups of people with different ways of thinking and working styles come together in an international team, they must establish a common way of working together. Tuckman calls this the *norming* stage of team development, after *forming* and *storming*. In this unit we will look at a key area of *norming*: setting clear roles and responsibilities for team members.

Setting clear roles and responsibilities

If a team member is unsure of what they have to do, or has a different expectation of their role to other team members, then teamwork can quickly become inefficient.

Across cultures there are very different ideas about team roles. For example, team members from individualistic cultures may see their primary role as achieving personal goals. Team members from more collectivist cultures may be more motivated to work together to reach common goals.

In some cultures roles and responsibilities may be very clearly defined, documented and tracked by a team leader. In others, team members may have a general framework with more freedom to reach the target in the way they want to – team leaders and members need to clarify this at the outset.

State expectations of roles

My role as leader of the IT sub-project is *to make sure we create a learning portal or platform on the website which can effectively communicate and promote the leadership training.* **I don't really see it as my role** *to develop the content of the portal, only the infrastructure.* **For me, your role is** *to deliver the content on time and I'll make sure we can launch by the end of the year.*

Then it's important to check to see if others in the team share these expectations.

How do you see my role? What are your expectations of my role in the project?

TRACK 57　Listen to a discussion between two people working in an international project within a cosmetics company to develop a new product. Ann is from Marketing and Mary is from Research and Development. How is Ann's role seen differently by the two team members? Why do they see her role so differently? What do you think will be the result of their discussion? You can read the audio script and check your answers on page 170.

How do you handle different expectations of team role in *your* working contexts?

Negotiate agreement on responsibilities individuals will take in the team

After clarifying how people see their role, individual team members have to take responsibility for specific tasks. At this point it may be necessary to give up some responsibilities and agree to new tasks and ways of working.

Accepting tasks: *I'll talk to Production to see if they have any problems, if you see that as my role.*

Giving up tasks: *OK, so you'll handle customer questions on technical matters, not me.*

Asking members to carry out new tasks: *Can you handle the issue of budgeting?*

Agreeing on processes: *I'll let you have a report every two weeks rather than every month.*

Read the email below from Ann to her project leader, Jane. What do you think the project leader will think about this email?

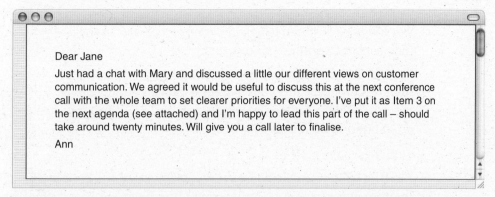

Dear Jane

Just had a chat with Mary and discussed a little our different views on customer communication. We agreed it would be useful to discuss this at the next conference call with the whole team to set clearer priorities for everyone. I've put it as Item 3 on the next agenda (see attached) and I'm happy to lead this part of the call – should take around twenty minutes. Will give you a call later to finalise.

Ann

🔊 **TRACK 58**   Listen to the telephone call Jane makes to Ann. Why is Jane unhappy? What does Jane ask Ann to do in future when she has ideas to discuss at meetings? You can read the audio script and check your answers on pages 170–1.

What do you see as the key responsibilities of the team leader? How far are these responsibilities only of the team leader, or how far can they be shared by all the team members?

In some cultures team members will be highly self-motivated to carry out their responsibilities without the need for a manager or colleagues to motivate them. In other cultures, team leaders may need to coach performance from team members and use positive feedback to motivate them, for example *You're doing a great job*. Without this encouragement, members of a virtual team may quickly become demotivated and begin to underperform in their roles.

What motivates you to perform well in your international teams? What other factors motivate your team colleagues? How far do you see it as your responsibility to coach and motivate performance in others?

HOT TIPS

- Define clearly how you see your role and responsibilities
- Check how others define your role and responsibilities and agree a common definition
- Support and motivate everyone in the team to perform well in their role (see Unit 43 on feedback and Unit 44 on coaching)

40 Getting the best out of your team

Tuckman's model shows very successful teams moving through *forming*, *storming* and *norming* to a final *performing* phase. In the *performing* phase team members are working well together.

In order for diverse international teams to become high-performing groups, it's important that the different opinions and ideas of team members are used to reach creative and effective solutions. Let's look at five ways to get the best out of an international team.

1 Listen to each other

Find out what team members are doing outside of the project team. They may, for example, be under a lot of pressure from their local line manager to deliver other projects which you don't know about.

🌐 **TRACK 59** Listen to a dinner conversation between Julika and Chris. What questions does Julika ask Chris about his manager back home? What important information does she discover? You can read the audio script and check your answers on page 171.

2 Make it easy for people to communicate

In any international team you may have a mixture of non-native and native speakers of English. It's important to make the non-native speakers comfortable with working in a second language. Use break-out groups frequently for discussion – people feel less pressure to speak in small groups than in large groups. Provide translations for key documentation.

🌐 **TRACK 60** Listen to a team meeting. What does Julika, the chair of the meeting, do to help the non-native speakers? You can read the audio script and check your answers on page 171.

3 Get people to think creatively together

Diverse teams can reach creative solutions if team members give their ideas freely. People should be encouraged to say what they think (Step 1) and to explore each other's opinions (Step 2) to reach the best solution.

Step 1: Encourage people to give opinions
John, I'm sure you have another view on this. What do you think?
Petra, you haven't said too much so far. What's your view?
Simon, what's the perspective of the UK business unit?

Step 2: Encourage investigation of each other's opinions

Petra. What did you think of Simon's idea?

Simon, what would Petra's suggestions mean in the UK context?

Before we dismiss Petra's solution, can we just spend a little time looking at how it could work?

🔊 **TRACK 61**   Listen to part of a telephone conference. What question does the leader of the conference ask which makes the team think about Christina's idea in more detail? You can read the audio script and check your answers on page 171.

What do you think about asking such a question? How far could it be too confrontational in some cultures?

4 Connect the best ideas together and take a decision

The final challenge is to take a decision that takes the best ideas given by different team members. The advantage of doing this is that people feel more committed to the final decision.

Simon, I think there's some overlap between your idea and what Petra mentioned. Can't we agree to ...?

If we take the ideas from Simon and Petra and put them together, couldn't we ...?

🔊 **TRACK 62**   Listen to a discussion between team colleagues over lunch. Which two ideas do they bring together to find a creative solution? You can read the audio script and check your answers on pages 171–2.

5 Celebrate effective teamwork

It's important to recognise team success when it happens. Feedback is an important way to develop a positive team spirit and to support cooperation, creativity and high performance.

I think we have a great solution which integrates many of the different views ...

Good work today. We had some great ideas and I'm sure that the decision we took will ...

Which of the above techniques would you like to use in *your* international team?

HOT TIPS

- Spend time in getting to know your team colleagues in order to collaborate effectively
- Create an open communication culture in the team
- Make use of the diverse opinions in the team to find creative solutions

International leadership

'A leader is best when people barely know he exists, when his work is done, his aim fulfilled, and when they will say: we did it ourselves.'

Lao Tzu

Leadership means different things to different people. Some people focus on leadership qualities – charisma, intelligence, integrity. Others highlight an understanding of human nature, technical excellence and experience. Others focus on actual behaviours – problem-solving, making decisions, getting people to do things, delegating.

In this module we focus on key areas of international leadership communication and stress three main principles:

1 There is no single 'right' approach to leadership. Instead, leaders should choose styles and behaviours which suit the people they are working with.

2 Those who are not leaders have to understand leadership. The more the principles and challenges of leadership are understood within an organisation, the more likely they are to be effective.

3 Those who are not leaders but who are working in international teams on projects have to show leadership qualities.

41 International leadership styles

Leadership is about working with people to achieve results. Effective international leaders need to lead with a range of styles which take into account the different talents, values and expectations of the people they are leading.

Adapt your leadership style to the individual

In the 1960s, Paul Hersey and Ken Blanchard developed a model of **situational leadership**. They describe four different leadership styles which should be used according to the abilities (competence) and the mindset (level of commitment) of the follower. Leaders assess the people they are leading in relation to specific tasks by using these two dimensions – **competence** and **commitment**. They then select the right leadership communication style.

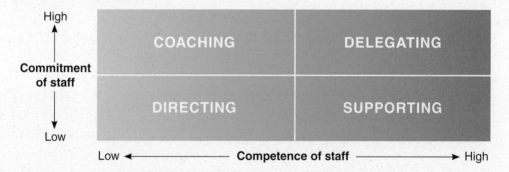

The four communication styles of situational leadership

1 Directing   For followers with low competence and low commitment to a specific task. Communication is one-way with the leader defining roles and tasks – telling the follower what to do – and closely supervising them while they do it.

Please finish the report by Friday. We need it to make a presentation to the Board.

2 Coaching   For followers with low competence but high commitment to completing the task. Communication is two-way, with the leader still directing and deciding what needs to be done, but also asking for ideas and suggestions from the follower.

When do you think you will finish the report? Do we need more information?

3 Supporting   For followers who can complete tasks competently, but who lack confidence or who are worried by risks. Communication is less about defining tasks – the follower has this competence – but more about giving advice, building motivation and confidence, and helping the follower to take the right decisions.

If you need help with the report, ask me or Roger. But I'm sure you can do it.

4 Delegating For followers who are experienced and motivated to complete the task independently. Communication is about giving high-level direction with further involvement and support of the leader to be decided *only* by the follower.

Any questions or anything I can help with?

🔊 TRACK 63 Listen to four short conversations between a leader and her staff members. Which leadership style is used in each conversation? You can read the audio script and check your answers on page 172.

1 .... 2 .... 3 .... 4 ....

In which situations in *your* work do you use the different styles described above? Which of the above styles do you prefer to lead with and be led by?

How to implement situational leadership effectively across cultures

Work in the culture, not against the culture
International leaders must consider broader cultural factors when managing individuals. Using the wrong style may damage personal credibility and confuse people. For example, if a directive leadership style is the cultural norm, it isn't sensible to use a delegating style.

Spend time with people
Leaders may sometimes find it difficult to spend enough time with people to fully assess levels of competence and commitment in their followers. Additionally, working in a foreign language may also make it difficult to properly assess real levels of engagement. However, effective international leaders find time to listen to people and to build their level of commitment.

Explain your leadership style
In order to clarify expectations about leadership, particularly within diverse teams where members don't share the same opinions about leadership, it's important for leaders to discuss their approach. Through discussion, they can establish common understanding and commitment on how to work together.

How would you describe *your* preferred leadership style? How useful would it be to discuss leadership styles with those you lead, and those who lead you?

HOT TIPS

Choose the most effective leadership approach for you based on:
- the skill levels and experience of the members of your team
- the cultural and business environment
- your own preferred style(s) which you present to and discuss with others

42 Communicating the way forward

A very important part of international leadership is to provide a clear and engaging vision of the future. The vision has to inspire people to work with focus and commitment towards strategic goals.

People can be engaged in different ways: some people will require information before they believe; others will only follow those who *do* rather than just say. Some will only believe in a leader who is charismatic; others will just want the independence to lead themselves.

How to create an engaging leadership vision

1 Convince with credible and powerful arguments

Employees are more likely to follow a leader who has the arguments to support his or her vision. Effective communicators use logic based on personal experience and competence.

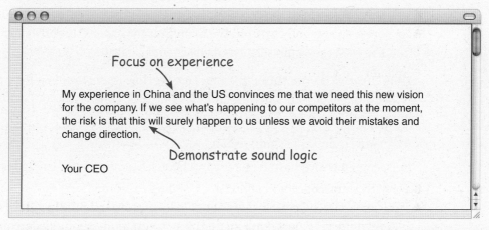

Focus on experience

My experience in China and the US convinces me that we need this new vision for the company. If we see what's happening to our competitors at the moment, the risk is that this will surely happen to us unless we avoid their mistakes and change direction.

Demonstrate sound logic

Your CEO

Which arguments do leaders in your organisation use to support the company or team vision? How far are you able to convince people: always – usually – sometimes – hardly ever – never?

2 Demand and deliver high standards

Leaders who promise and deliver high performance themselves can inspire loyalty and commitment to their vision.

🎧 **TRACK 64** Listen to a team leader in a conference call describing a promise that he has just kept. What promise was made and what was delivered? You can read the audio script and check your answers on page 172.

How important is it in *your* work to make and deliver on personal promises?

3 Focus on values

International leaders who state their commitment to common values and then live these values, for example by listening to people and showing openness, can also get support.

🎵 **TRACK 65** Listen to an extract from the presentation of a project sponsor at the kick-off meeting of her project. Which value does she stress when delivering her vision? You can read the audio script and check your answers on pages 172–3.

Which values are important for leaders to stress in *your* organisation?

4 Show people how they can support the vision

Visions can fail if they aren't connected to the daily life of ordinary workers. Effective leaders can successfully motivate employees by showing how everyday effort in the office supports the wider organisation's strategy.

🎵 **TRACK 66** Listen to an international project leader giving a motivational speech to his team at the beginning of a three-day kick-off event. Which corporate strategy does he tell the team that their work directly supports? You can read the audio script and check your answers on page 173.

How effective do you think this message is? How important is it for you to understand how your work and the work of your colleagues connect to the bigger picture of corporate strategy?

5 Stress common responsibility

For people to work hard to achieve a vision, they need to take responsibility. Leaders, therefore, should emphasise the idea that *everyone* is responsible for realising the vision – it isn't simply a leader's task, but a common leadership responsibility.

🎵 **TRACK 67** Listen to a project leader describing her role and the concept of responsibility she has for the project. Who does she see as the leader of this project? You can read the audio script and check your answers on page 173.

How acceptable would it be to communicate a message of shared leadership in *your* working contexts?

HOT TIPS
- Connect your vision to your organisation's strategy
- Stress shared responsibility for achieving the vision
- Repeat the vision frequently in formal presentations and during informal conversations to clarify and to persuade

43 Giving and getting feedback

Giving and getting feedback on work performance can reduce misunderstanding and miscommunication created by cultural diversity.

Feedback across cultures

International leaders need to understand different styles of feedback across cultures and to develop a range of styles suitable for the different contexts and individuals they are working with. Look at the summary below.

- In some contexts feedback is given top-down by the manager to the staff member. In others, there is a bottom-up approach, with the staff member giving feedback.

- In some contexts feedback focuses on the positive – what went well. In others, it focuses more on the negative – what went wrong and has to be improved.

- In some contexts very direct feedback is appreciated. In others, a more indirect 'sensitive' and positive approach is used.

- In some contexts feedback is very frequent and informal. In others, it is infrequent – perhaps only once a year – and is part of a formal process.

- In some contexts feedback is given in private on a one-to-one basis. In others, it can take place with the whole team present.

What is the feedback style in *your* culture? Which style(s) do you use?

How to GIVE feedback

Here are some general principles for giving effective feedback. They should be adapted to specific cultural contexts.

- Start feedback positively in order that people are truly open to the process.
  Let me just start by saying that I think you've done a great job this year.

- Ask questions to make people reflect on their own behaviour and performance, positives and negatives.
  What do you think about your performance last year? What went well, what not so well?

- Focus on the consequences of a person's behaviour.
  When you were late with the proposal, the customer was very angry.

- Identify new behaviours which will have a positive impact.
  Ask: *What will you do differently next time?* (see Coaching in Unit 44)
  Tell: *I think you need to inform the customer if you are going to be late.*

- Agree what to do and how to measure progress.
  OK, so you'll keep in contact more regularly with the customer and I'll check informally if the customer is happy around once a month.
- Get feedback on your feedback.
  How was the feedback session today? What did you like? What can we improve?

How effective would these feedback principles be in *your* work?

How to GET feedback

It's vital that everyone working internationally – leaders and followers – ask for feedback from their partners. Feedback enables people to understand how others see and think about them, and to identify areas of improvement. Here are some ideas to help you get good feedback.

- Build the getting of feedback into your regular leadership communication.
  Could you give me some quick feedback on how I handled that meeting?
- Be open. Don't argue or justify yourself when someone gives you feedback. Listen and check on which of your behaviours caused a problem.
- Accept the feedback as important *information* rather than the 'truth'. It's the opinion of the person giving it, and it's interesting to hear and understand what people think about your actions.
- Think about the feedback and choose what you want to do with it – accept it or reject it, do something about it or do nothing.
- Where you feel the feedback is relevant and accurate, create a plan of action to help you develop better performance.

TRACK 68   Listen to part of a meeting where an international leader gives feedback to a member of her team, Peter, about the organisation of a sales conference for customers. Which customer group has given negative feedback, and why? How happy is Peter with the feedback? You can read the audio script and check your answers on page 173.

HOT TIPS

- Create a feedback plan that identifies who you should give feedback to, who you should get feedback from, and how often
- Practise giving and getting feedback frequently
- Use the feedback to improve your own behaviour

44 Coaching

Coaching is a process of supporting others to solve problems and to develop themselves. Many large international organisations now invest in coaching training for their leaders. In this unit we look at a coaching model which consists of a set of communication tools based around listening and asking questions. Managers can use this model to help those who report to them in their daily work.

The D-R-I-V-E model

This can be used to structure meetings between coach and coachee (the person being coached). It has five main phases with questions encouraging the coachee to reflect and find creative solutions to problems.

D Define the objective (Phase 1)

At the beginning of a coaching session, coaches should take time to understand the needs and expectations of the coachee and, eventually, to define objectives for the meeting.

What shall we focus on today? | What's your objective for our meeting?

🎧 **TRACK 69**   Listen to the beginning of a coaching session. What does the coachee identify as the objective? Which open question is used by the coach to move from phase 1 to phase 2? You can read the audio script and check your answers on pages 174–5.

How well do you think the coach opens the dialogue? How might you do it differently?

R Reflect on causes and possible solutions (Phase 2)

In the next phase the coach uses questions to explore the background to the issue and possible solutions to it. Questions should be open, and help the coachee to find new ideas for dealing with the specific challenge.

What have you tried? | How does your colleague see this issue? | What else could you do?

🎧 **TRACK 70**   Listen to more of the coaching session. What does the coachee identify as the cause of the problem? Which open question is used by the coach to move from phase 2 to phase 3 below? You can read the audio script and check your answers on page 174.

I   Initiate a plan (Phase 3)

In this phase the coachee is asked to identify concrete action steps which will help to resolve the issue in some way.

So, what's your action plan? | So, what would you like to do next? | What needs to happen now?

🎧 TRACK 71   Listen to the same coaching session as coach and coachee move to define an action plan. How do the coach's questions support the coachee in this conversation? You can read the audio script and check your answers on page 174.

V   View obstacles (Phase 4)

Coaches should encourage coachees to consider obstacles or risks that may stop them implementing their action plan. In this phase, the coach can ask the coachee to identify the risks and think of actions or people who can give support to manage the risks.

What might stop you from reaching your objective? | Who can help you? | Who stands in your way?

🎧 TRACK 72   Listen to this phase of the session. What obstacle is identified and what solution is proposed? You can read the audio script and check your answers on pages 174–5.

E   Evaluate progress (Phase 5)

The final phase is to summarise the conversation and agree to a future meeting to evaluate progress. The last question should be to get feedback on the coaching session itself.

So, can you summarise what we discussed? | When should we meet to evaluate progress? | How useful was our session today?

🎧 TRACK 73   Listen to the final phase of the coaching session. What does the coachee say was most useful about the coaching style of the coach? You can read the audio script and check your answers on page 175.

HOT TIPS

- When coaching others, use open questions to drive the process
- When coaching, make sure you get commitment to a clear action plan at the end of the coaching dialogue
- As a coachee, see coaching as an opportunity to develop new skills and a better understanding of yourself

45 Building trust across cultures

It is a leadership responsibility to build trust at work. As a leader, you need to make it possible for others to trust you; you also need to trust others. Without trust, information does not flow freely across organisations, expensive controls are necessary to check on staff, leading potentially to lower motivation and to lower performance.

Here we present ten dimensions of trust and look at how to use them in work situations to make others trust your leadership. These ten dimensions of trust will have a different importance in different cultures. Effective leaders understand which dimensions are effective in which culture, and when and how to communicate these dimensions when they talk to people.

Ten dimensions of trust

1 Trust me because I'm good at my job

Follower I'm not sure how to solve this. Shall I contact the IT department?
Leader No, I think I know how to solve it.

2 Trust me because I'm similar to you

It's important to identify and communicate common values, interests, objectives and experiences which you have with international contacts.

Follower Have you worked on a major IT project before?
Leader Yes, I was part of an SAP software roll-out in my previous company.
Follower Really?
Leader Yes, so we both have a lot of experience of this area.

3 Trust me because I care about you

Caring is about showing empathy, support and commitment towards others.

Leader Jan, you look a little bit tired.
Follower Yes, my son is very ill today and missed school.
Leader Why don't you finish work early today? You should be at home.

4 Trust me because I have integrity

People who have integrity have ethical principles which guide their behaviour.

Leader I'm sorry, but I'm not nominating you for promotion this year.
Follower Why not?
Leader Well, I want to be honest and say that I don't think you're ready for it this year. But as I always tell you, you do have the potential.
Follower OK, thanks for being so honest.

5 Trust me because I'm reliable and consistent

Followers need to trust that leaders will deliver on promises.

Leader   Don't worry about resources. You can rely on me to get additional budget and people if we need them. As I said at the beginning of the project, and I'll say it again and again, just get on with completing your tasks on time. I'll get you any extra resources you need as long as you can show me that you really need them.

6 Trust me because I'm not competing against you

Trust is able to develop when people feel secure with international leaders and don't see them as a threat to their local organisation.

Leader   I know I'm from the headquarters but I'm here to support your local business unit. My priority is to guarantee jobs, not take work away from you. I want to support you in running your own organisation effectively so that I can move on to the next challenge.

7 Trust me because I keep you involved

Effective leaders keep people involved at all times. Without involvement, commitment can begin to decrease and results become more difficult to achieve.

Leader   I'd appreciate it if you could attend the meeting next week. We need your input to decide where to locate the new factory. Have you had any thoughts on this at all?

8 Trust me because I share information

It's good to share information, but don't overload followers with too much.

Leader   Hello, it's Stefano. Just a quick call. Have you spoken to Geoff about the Telco project?
Follower Not recently. Why?
Leader   Geoff and I got an email this morning which suggested that there are technical problems in production in China. So I just wanted to let you know as soon as possible that a delay is likely.
Follower That's great. If there is going to be a delay it means I don't need to meet the board this morning to ask for approval for my marketing plan. Thanks for the information.

9 Trust me because I'm open with my feelings

Trust is an emotional process. By opening up and sharing feelings, you can help followers to develop trust.

Follower   Is this delay going to be a problem?
Leader   To be honest, I'm really worried. This will cause a lot of difficulties.

10 Trust me because I trust you

It's impossible to ask for trust from others when you don't show trust back. Show trust by giving people responsibilities and not controlling too closely if the tasks have been completed to right quality.

Leader   Have you finished that proposal yet?
Follower   Yes, would you like to see it before I send it to the customer?
Leader   No, that's not necessary. I'm sure it's fine.

How far do *you* show trust by giving people extra responsibilities?

HOT TIPS

- Build the ten dimensions of trust into your conversations with people
- Adapt your trust-building strategy to specific individuals and the cultural / business context
- Take responsibility and be the first to start the trust-building process

Language reference

'Language is the means of getting an idea from my brain into yours without surgery.' Mark Amidon

In international business we use the English language to build relationships, to influence, to manage conflict, to take decisions together and to support each other over the longer term. These people-centred communication skills are at the centre of effective international collaboration.

In this module we provide a bank of phrases and sentences you can use to interact with people across cultures successfully. But remember, this language is for reference only. It's only a starting point for thinking about the specific things you want to say to specific people in your specific intercultural business situations.

Hopefully, these five units will provide you with language which will help you to get your message across successfully in the future.

46 English for building relationships

Review the language below when planning your relationship-building strategy. Then use or adapt the ideas and phrases for your specific international contacts, or simply use your own expressions.

Getting started

The relationship-building process starts the moment a new contact walks through the door into your office. The following framework provides a useful starting point from which you can lead conversations effectively.

Introductions

Good morning. My name is ... Welcome to ...
Good to see you (again). How are you?
OK. Please follow me. We can go to my office.

Polite offers

May I take your coat?
Can I get you something to drink? Tea? Coffee? Juice?
Please, take a seat.
I hope you're free for dinner tonight?

Polite questions about travel

Did you have a good trip?
How was the flight? Everything on time?
Did you have any problems finding us?
Is everything OK with the hotel?
Is this your first time in ...?
So, have you been travelling much this year?

Polite questions about work

What are you working on at the moment?
How's business at the moment?
Are you busy with the Telcom project? I heard it's going well.
How is the reorganisation going? I heard it's a tough process.

Build a bond by exploring common people networks

You know John Hansen, don't you? How is he?
Have you heard anything about Jean-Claude?
Is Peter still working with you in the project?

Developing the conversation

You can develop conversations in many different ways. The following approach consists of three key phases:

1 looking for a subject to talk about
2 developing the topic with open questions
3 finding common experiences to create a feeling of mutual understanding.

Looking for a subject

So, do you have any experience of …?
Have you ever been to …?

Developing the topic

When will you … | Why did you … | How do you … | What are you …?

Finding common experiences

So, you also …
Did you have the same experience?
How did you find it? Was it similar?
Your background is IT? Mine too. What kind of IT work?

Getting down to business

Task-oriented individuals will prefer to get down to business quite quickly, and perhaps develop interpersonal rapport later during lunch or dinner. With these people you probably won't spend much time with the phrases above. You can use the following language to begin the business discussion almost immediately.

Beginning the meeting formally

I think we can get right down to business, if that's fine with you.
We have a lot of things to get through today. Let's get started.
We need to take some important decisions today. Shall we start?

HOT TIPS

- Get the relationship-building process moving with basic introductions and routine questions about travel and work
- Keep the conversation going by asking a range of open questions
- Adapt your relationship-building style to the needs of your international partner. Observe and adapt

47 English for influencing

Review the language below when planning your influencing strategy. Then use or adapt the ideas and phrases for your specific international contacts and projects, or simply use your own expressions.

'Push' style of influencing – four steps

1 Explain the facts	*Firstly, let's look at the facts.* *We have to accept the fact that …*
2 Introduce clear proposals	*My strong belief is that …* *This data clearly shows that …*
3 Deal with objections strongly	*To be honest, that argument is wrong.* *What you said is not correct because …*
4 Pressure people to agree	*So, I think we can agree to …* *Are we are ready to decide …?*

'Pull' style of influencing – four steps

1 Introduce your view	*As I see it, …* *May I start with my view on …?*
2 Listen to others	*What's your opinion?* *How do you see this?*
3 Find a compromise	*Could we agree to …?* *Would you be willing to …?*
4 Agree a 'win-win' compromise	*So, if you … then we will …* *It's a win-win scenario if we …*

Influencing factors

1 Stress the benefits	*The main advantage for you is …* *This would enable you to …*
2 Cultivate trust in your expertise	*In my experience, we need to …* *This worked very well in the States.*
3 Be transparent	*I think there are two main arguments …* *The reason I think this is …*
4 Use logical arguments	*If we look at the data, you can see …* *The logical conclusion is to …*
5 Focus on the relationship	*I understand what you're saying …* *We've worked together a long time …*

6	Be strong	*There is simply no other solution.*
		It would be a mistake not to implement …
7	Look to the future	*My vision is …*
		The forecast is that …
8	Be confident	*I have no doubt that …*
		I am convinced that …
9	Show optimism	*I'm very positive about this because …*
		This should be no problem.

Be prepared

One of the most important influencing strategies is to prepare good counter-arguments to deal with objections. If you can respond quickly with good arguments, you'll come across as knowledgeable and as someone to be trusted.

Look at the list of objections and possible counter-arguments. Remember, these are only ideas to help you prepare for your specific situations.

Possible objections	Possible counter-arguments
Power play	Escalate
I cannot authorise this.	*OK, but then we need to ask my manager.*
Fear of failure	Focus on opportunity
What if this goes wrong?	*If we do this, it will enable us to …*
Experience	Differentiate then and now
We've done this before.	*But now the situation is different because …*
Moral	Argue it *is* moral
This isn't ethical.	*I'm convinced this is ethical because …*
Priorities	Stress risks
I have more important tasks.	*OK, but if we don't do this, then …*
Analysis	Push people to be specific
We need more information.	*What do you need to know exactly?*
Lack of understanding	Be patient and go back to the beginning
I don't understand.	*Perhaps I should go over this again.*

HOT TIPS

- Choose a 'push' or 'pull' style, depending on the cultural and business context
- Think about which influencing factors will impact on the person you have to talk to
- Make sure you have counter-arguments prepared for any possible objections

48 English for taking decisions

Review the language below when planning how to handle decision-making discussions and meetings. Then use or adapt the ideas and phrases for your specific international contacts, or simply use your own expressions.

Starting a decision-making meeting

Remember, decision-making styles can differ enormously in terms of:

- roles – who is responsible for the decision?
- information – how much do we need to know before we take a decision?
- time frame – how urgent is the decision?

It's extremely important to begin a decision-making discussion with clear agreement on objectives, process and roles. If these areas aren't clarified, it's possible to waste a lot of time in the meeting.

Beginning positively

As you all know, the objective of the meeting today is to look at the …
Let's turn to the issue of …, which I'm sure we can find a solution to.
Right, our next challenge is to work together to solve the issue of …

Explaining the challenge with simple words

I think there's one major issue.
Basically, we have to solve …
I've divided the problem into three main areas. Firstly, … Secondly, … Finally, …

Identifying common objectives

Although we may disagree on details, I think we're all agreed that …
I think there are a number of different views on this problem but I'm confident …
We all need a solution to this issue because …

Explaining the decision-making process

Can we start with …?
In terms of the process today, I'd like to begin with …
Can we begin with … and then move on to …?

Defining decision timeframes

How soon do we need to take a decision on this?
When do you need a decision?
I think we can decide when we …

Setting criteria

Our decision should be based on …
On what basis will we take our decision?
The deciding factor will be …

Defining roles

I want this to be very much a group decision, so everyone should feel free to …
We need to involve …
… will take the final decision.

Taking a decision

Across cultures there are many different ways to give opinions and find agreement. Different expectations of directness or indirectness can lead to conflict in discussions, so it's important to communicate in a way which our partners feel is respectful.

Discussing options

What do you think we should do?
Which option is best for you?
In my opinion we should decide to …

Disagreeing

I think this would cause a problem because …
I can't agree to this because …
I don't think this will work.

Pushing to a decision

Can we come to a decision?
I think we need to take a decision now.
Does this means we have agreement?

Agreeing

Good idea.
I have no problem with this. It's a good solution.
I can agree to this if …

Confirming decisions

Never assume that there is common understanding or full agreement after a discussion. It's always useful in a meeting to summarise, confirm decisions and next steps, and to use written minutes as a support.

Summarising

Let me just go over what we've decided.
To summarise, we've decided to …
OK, we'll … . Agreed?

Creating an action plan

Can we agree an action plan?
Who will do what?
When do we need to …?

Closing

I'll circulate the minutes so that everyone can sign.
Good. Any other comments?
I think we can close here.

Taking decisions across cultures is a complex process. Problems with language mean that people may agree to something in the meeting they didn't fully understand. Differences in communication style mean that 'yes' may not mean full agreement or commitment. It's advisable to telephone key people after decision-making meetings to clarify again and to confirm full commitment to any decision.

HOT TIPS

- Take time to structure the decision-making process at the beginning of a meeting
- Make sure you express differences of opinion in a style which is clear and respectful to your international partners
- Take time after the decision-making meeting to get in touch with the participants to clarify and confirm commitment

49 English for managing conflict

Review the language below when handling meetings dealing with sensitive discussions or issues involving conflict. Then use or adapt the ideas and phrases for your specific international contacts, or simply use your own expressions.

Getting started

It's often very useful to create clear and positive ground rules at the beginning of any discussion of a sensitive issue.

Clarify the agenda and timetable

So, the objective today is to …
What we need to do today is …

Acknowledge the conflict

People feel very differently about …
There have been some problems …

Open with optimism

I'm very confident that we can find a solution today.
I've no doubt that we can solve this.

Focus on professional responsibility and common ground

We need to find a solution which enables us to work efficiently together.
As professionals, we need to solve …

State clearly the need to respect others

Let's try to show respect for each other in the meeting.
We need to listen to each other during …

Invite others to start

Shall we start by …?
I think it would be good to start by hearing …

Managing the discussion

One of the main challenges here is to keep the discussion focused and constructive.

Seek to understand the real issue with questions

How do you see the situation?
Why do you say that?

Surface different points of view

I think there are different ways to see this.
John has a different view of the situation. He sees it more as a question of …

Acknowledge the feelings of others

I understand that you feel …
Yes, and we should also consider how others feel.

Postpone the controversial

Maybe we should come back to this.
Let's move on to another topic for the moment …

Generate ideas

How far do you think it's possible to …?
I understand what you're saying. Are there other options?

Summarise frequently

Do does this mean that …?
So just to summarise, this means …

Finding a solution

It's important to move towards a shared solution which all parties commit to. At the end of the meeting it's important to summarise and confirm clear outcomes. It's also useful to celebrate success if conflict has been resolved. This creates a strong platform to move forward into the future.

Create general agreement and shared responsibility for a solution

So can we agree to both take responsibility for …
OK, do we commit to …?

Take time to celebrate success and reaffirm working relationships

Excellent. Well, I think we've done a good job. Well done.
That was a tough meeting but I think we've reached a very good conclusion.

HOT TIPS

- Begin the meeting with clear ground rules in order to keep things positive
- Remain calm even when people are using communication behaviours which you find challenging
- Work towards a solution which all parties can commit to

50 English for coaching

The D-R-I-V-E model uses an approach to coaching where the main role of the coach is to help the coachee to think of ideas to solve a real problem, and commit to an action plan with clear measures and a deadline. It is action-oriented coaching.

Here we give more ideas for questions which you could ask when you are acting as a coach. As always, use or adapt the ideas and phrases to your own business contexts, or simply use your own language.

The D-R-I-V-E model

D Define the objective (Phase 1)

At the beginning of a coaching session, the coach asks questions which encourage the coachee to define an objective for the coaching dialogue.

What shall we focus on today?
What's your objective for our meeting?
What's on your mind?
Where would you like to go with this?
What do you want to get out of this session?
What are you looking for from today?
Which of these issues is most urgent?
What would you like to change in this situation?
What would be a good focus for today?
It sounds like you're a little bit frustrated. What needs to change?

R Reflect on causes and possible solutions (Phase 2)

In the next phase the coach uses questions to explore the issue and possible solutions. Questions should stimulate the coachee to think creatively and find new possible solutions.

What have you already tried?
How successful was it?
What might work best now?
What else could you try?
What would happen as a result?
If you were brave, what would you do?
How would your colleague deal with this?
What do you think is missing in this situation?
So what needs to happen?

I   Initiate a plan (Phase 3)

In this phase the coachee should identify concrete action steps.

So, what's your action plan?
What needs to happen now?
What's the critical thing to do here now?
So, what should you do next?
What would the outcome of this approach be?
How will these actions achieve your goal?

V   View obstacles (Phase 4)

In this phase the coachee should consider obstacles or risks which might prevent them from reaching their objective.

What's stopping you?
What might prevent you from reaching your objective?
What are the problems you know, or can expect?
Who's standing in your way?
Who can help you?
What resources could you need?
What else might you need?
How realistic is all this?
If this is a barrier, what can you do about it?
What else needs to change to make this achievable?
Who will you need to involve to help you?

E   Evaluate progress (Phase 5)

The final phase is to summarise and agree to a future meeting to evaluate progress.

So, can you summarise what we discussed?
When should we meet to evaluate progress?
What are you going to do in the next few weeks?
How realistic is all this?
What will you do by when?
At our next meeting, how should we check progress?
What did you learn today?
How useful was our session today?
How do you feel after our conversation?

Coaching isn't simply a leadership tool. It's also a general mindset which supports three important principles:

1 I want to help others.

2 Communication is a process which I need to manage.

3 I can manage the communication process by asking rather than telling.

These three principles are not only action-oriented coaching principles, they are important intercultural principles. Coaching skills are intercultural skills. If we can adopt a coach-approach at the right time when working internationally, we will be more successful intercultural communicators.

HOT TIPS

- Use coaching behaviours to help and develop others
- Spend more time asking and less time telling

Conclusion

'Diversity is the one true thing we all have in common. Celebrate it every day.' Anon

Congratulations! You've made it to the end of the book. As a result, you now have a greater understanding of the term 'culture' and what it means for working internationally.

You will now be more sensitive to key dimensions of cultural diversity, and you will also be more aware of yourself and your impact on others.

You will have many more ideas on how to manage cultural differences and to communicate effectively across cultures.

Now the real work begins, as you start to transfer all these ideas into your daily international working life. This transfer will require effort and you will need to get ongoing feedback from those around you to ensure you can accelerate your progress as much as possible. We're confident that you can do it. You should be too.

Answer key and audio scripts

Profiling your international working style

Page 9

1 Meeting new people

Yes: Your working style is strongly people-oriented. You may have the ability to build rapport quickly with a range of people. However, people who are strongly task-oriented may think you spend too much time on small talk and not enough on getting the job done.

No: Your working style is strongly task-oriented. You may have the ability to focus quickly, and to focus groups quickly, on tasks when under time pressure. However, some people may find your approach a little impolite if you don't spend the time and make the effort to get to know them.

2 Being flexible

Yes: Your working style is based on a strong people orientation and a preference for harmony in working relationships. You may have the ability to make others feel comfortable with you by adapting to their style. However, some people may find it difficult to trust you if they see you changing your behaviours too much.

No: Your working style is based on being honest and authentic – being who you really are, rather than the person someone else wants you to be. You may have the ability to create trust in this way, as people will believe that what you say is what you really think. However, people may also feel uncomfortable with your behaviour at times and see you as inflexible in some circumstances.

3 Focusing on objectives

Yes: Your working style is strongly results-oriented. You may have the ability to reach your goals even in very difficult situations. However, some people may see you as too focused on your own goals and not able to negotiate compromises with those who have a different opinion.

No: Your working style is less focused on individual goals and more on reaching results which are right for the whole organisation. You may have the ability to see the bigger picture and negotiate with those who have a different opinion. However, some

people may think you lack focus on your own goals and that you are too easily influenced by others.

4 Dealing with change

Yes: You feel comfortable in situations where things are open and unplanned. You may have a strong wish to learn many new skills, rather than specialise and be expert on one area. Some people may think you lack focus at times, especially those who are experts and / or those who like to plan in detail.

No: You are someone who likes to organise and plan in order to be effective at work. You may prefer to be an expert in one subject rather than someone who learns a little about many topics. Some people, particularly in management, may see this way of working as problematic for international situations where tolerance of ambiguity is essential.

5 Understanding how others see me

Yes: You have a good understanding of your own working style and of how others will interpret it – either positively or negatively. You may have the ability to be flexible and adapt your style to make other people feel comfortable. However, you may spend too much time worrying about the opinion of other people rather than getting the job done.

No: You focus on getting the job done rather than on managing people's feelings. You may have the ability to remain calm during moments of conflict. You do not allow the emotions of others to influence your decision-making. However, you may not see that some people find parts of your working style difficult. As a result, you may slow down the process of relationship-building necessary for reaching a business result.

6 Listening effectively

Yes: You are someone who thinks that it is very important to clarify frequently what people say to you. You may ask a lot of questions to make sure that you understand their opinions. Some people may think that asking a lot of questions in this way shows a lack of expertise in the subject, and so may think you are not competent.

No: You are someone who believes that they can understand quickly what others are saying. You may prefer spending less time on communication and more time on doing things. However, you may misunderstand other people more often than you think. In addition, people may think you are a bad listener if you do not spend time commenting on and clarifying what they say to you.

7 Speaking clearly

Yes: You are a person who is sensitive to the challenges of communicating internationally in a foreign language. You have the ability to manage the way you speak to make sure that people can understand you – by speaking slowly, by simplifying your language, by explaining your reasons explicitly. However, some may think that your simplified communication style is too soft or not dynamic enough.

No: You may be a natural communicator who is able to get messages across easily. You may not need to simplify or moderate your way of speaking. However, some people may find your communication style problematic. It could be that international partners frequently misinterpret the meaning of what you say: for example, a request is seen as an order.

8 Understanding cultures

Yes: You believe that it is important to know about the cultures of your international partners. You may have the ability to build respect by showing this knowledge during business conversations. However, you may focus too much on knowledge rather than on adapting your own behaviour.

No: You feel it is more important to know the individual than to learn about the culture. You may have the ability to form strong interpersonal relationships without knowing much about the wider cultural context. However, without this knowledge you may manage people in the wrong way or take poor decisions.

9 Influencing decisions

Yes: Your working style is based on networking with a wide range of people. You understand that many decisions in international organisations are very political. You know that if you want to influence a decision, you have to get close to key decision-makers. However, some people may see this kind of management behaviour as too political and begin to mistrust what you say to them.

No: Your working style is focused on results. You are not interested in playing political games with senior managers who have influence on key decisions. However, some people may think you are a little naive for international working. You may not have the skills to build enough influence with key decision-makers to enable you to get what you want.

10 Managing diversity

Yes: You see diversity as an advantage. You analyse the different working styles in the people around you, and you allocate tasks according to specific competence. In meetings, you make sure that different opinions are heard and evaluated. However, some people may think the time you take to collect different opinions shows a lack of leadership.

No: You see it as your role to lead and to give direction. You may think that differences are best managed by creating common guidelines which everyone can follow. However, you may not spend enough time listening to different opinions which could produce innovative solutions.

Module one

Unit 3   page 18

1 b, d   2 c, d   3 b, c   4 a, b, c   5 a, b, c

Module two

Unit 7   page 30

(*Value orientations*)

1 Human nature: white

2 Person vs. Nature: light yellow

3 Time: dark grey

4 Activity: light grey

5 Relational: dark yellow

page 30

(*Extract from a business meeting*)

One possible answer is that Angela shows more sensitivity in giving her opinion less directly, signalling to Bob her understanding of his position. Bob, however, expresses his opinions directly and forcefully, and is not very sensitive to Angela's point of view.

On the other hand, you could also say that Angela is not very sensitive to that fact that she may have to give her opinions more powerfully in order to convince Bob that she is right.

TRACK 2

Caroline   So, what do you think we should do, Bob?

Bob   Well, it's clear to me. We need to invest in better software to stop these problems happening again. And we need to do this fast.

Angela   Well, I'm not sure. Maybe we need to take a little bit more time to look into things.

Bob   Take time? Why? We know the problem and we know the solution. Let's just do it.

Caroline   Yes, erm … maybe Angela has a different view on this.

Angela   Yes, I see what you mean, Bob, but I think the current software is pretty good in many respects.

Bob   Oh, come on. It's created so many problems in the last few months. I think we need to make a change immediately!

Unit 10   page 39

Possible answers include:

(*Description*)

There is a group of people.

The two people at the front are wearing shorts and T-shirts.

Some of the people are holding their arms out in front of them.

(*Interpretation*)

The people are dancing at an open air music festival.

The two boys are taking part in some form of competition.

A teacher – out of the picture – is teaching this crowd of people a special dance. *

* Real explanation: *European New Zealanders learn indigenous dance moves at a cultural workshop at a music festival in New Plymouth.*

(*Evaluation*)

It's a nice picture because people are having fun. I don't like this picture. I hate dancing in public and this reminds me of that.

page 40

He has decided to do it the same way. He expects he will feel more relaxed.

TRACK 3

(*Description*)

I gave a two-hour presentation to the client this morning. Nobody said a single word during the whole of the two hours. And at the end I only had one or maybe two questions. Everyone was looking at me but nobody was smiling or even nodding. I got very little feedback from the audience before I left.

(*Interpretation*)

In the UK, presentation audiences normally participate a little, if only to make the presenter feel more comfortable – just with occasional comments or questions. It's actually polite to give some form of positive feedback at the end. My host told me after the presentation that for him it's respectful to be silent. Positive feedback is given by saying nothing. I'd only get feedback – and then negative feedback – if I said something wrong.

(*Evaluation*)

I first felt very uncomfortable in the situation. After a few minutes I even became a little irritated because I felt the audience were aggressive towards me. But once I understood what the behaviour of the audience meant, then I felt good. The presentation had gone well and we got orders from the client. Next time, I'll probably do the presentation in the same way – people seemed happy – but I'll feel much more relaxed.

Module three

Unit 11   page 43

Part 1

What they said

American: How long will it take you to finish this report?

Greek: I don't know. How long should it take?

American: You're in the best position to analyse time requirements.

Greek: Ten days.

American: Take 15. Is it agreed you'll do it in 15 days?

What they were thinking

American: I believe in participatory management. I want him to take responsibility for this task so I ask him a question rather than just telling him what to do.

Greek: He's my boss. He should tell me what to do so I ask him for his opinion on how long the task should take.

American: I push him to take responsibility for the task by repeating the question.

Greek: I don't really understand the question but I'll give him an answer to keep him happy.

American: I'm happy that he has given an answer but he has not estimated enough time so I will give him more. I push for a commitment – a verbal contract – that he agrees to do the report in 15 days. This is our deal.

Part 2

What they said

American: Where is my report?

Greek: It will be ready tomorrow.

American: But we had agreed that it would be ready today.

Greek: This is unacceptable. I resign.

What they were thinking

American: I ask a question to check if he has honoured his contract and completed the report.

Greek: I haven't had time to finish the complex report. I inform my boss of a little delay.

American: I'm unhappy. We had a contract to complete the report by today. I expect my employee to take more responsibility when they commit to an action.

Greek: This boss has no understanding of all the hard work which I have put in to try to complete this report. Not one word of positive feedback. I can't work for him. I have to leave.

Unit 12   page 45

3 Per-Erik comments that his company has a long experience in providing brand solutions in the retail sector.

🔘 **TRACK 4**

Alan   So what we're looking for is a website designer who can really help us to brand ourselves a little more clearly.
Per-Erik   Brand?
Alan   Yes, we have a brand but I think we need support to create a clearer message.
Per-Erik   I agree with you. Today brand is everything. Without a strong brand you will lose ground to your competitors. And listening to you, I think we have the right experience because we've been working to develop clear and strong brands with our customers, particularly in retail, for the last ten years.
Alan   That sounds good. If you have such a long experience in the retail sector, it sounds like you could be a good partner for us.

page 46

6 The listener, C, in the second conversation is more effective. He shows understanding and concern for the speaker and offers support. The listener, A, in the first conversation does not sympathise with the stressful situation of the speaker and, at the end of the conversation, switches the topic to her own experience.

🔘 **TRACK 5**

A   Hi, John. How are you doing?
B   Oh, not so good. I've got a lot of work on at the moment and I have to travel to Moscow next week.
A   Moscow? Sounds nice. I'd love to go there.

B   Yes, but it's only in and out of a meeting room and a hotel room so …

A   Oh, you'll have time to see a few things surely?

B   Erm, not really because …

A   Yes, I remember when I was in Moscow last year. It was really nice. We spent a bit of time …

C   Hi, Jackie. How are you doing?

D   Oh, really busy at the moment. I'm working on this Telco project. It's quite tough.

C   I can imagine. I heard some stories about it. Is it stressful?

D   Yes, very! The project goals are still not really that clear and we don't have enough resources.

C   That must be tough. Can I help at all?

D   Thanks but not really. To be honest, what I need is a holiday so that I can just …

page 46

8   The presenter explains that she feels quality is more important than following the schedule.

🎧 TRACK 6

A   Are there any questions at this point?

B   Yes, you mentioned that the project was behind schedule. Is it bad news for you that the project will deliver late?

A   This is a very good question, and it's important for everyone in this room to hear the answer. For me, quality is more important than schedule. Of course, I want projects to finish on time but I would rather have the right quality than the wrong quality on schedule. So I need all of you in this project to deliver quality results and not just results on time.

Unit 13   page 47

The speaker shows a positive attitude in dialogue 2. He gives the speaker time for the conversation even when he is in a hurry. He also checks what is said to create clear understanding.

In dialogue 1, the listener does not see the speaker's message as important because she has no time. In dialogue 3, the listener lacks patience and becomes confused and frustrated with the rather complex speaking style of the speaker.

🎧 TRACK 7

Dialogue 1

A   So, what do you think about my recommendation on pricing?

B   What, oh sorry. Erm, look … I'm not sure I'm the right person to answer this.

A   But you're in charge of marketing, aren't you? So what I need is …

B   Yes, but I'm really busy now. Can we discuss this tomorrow or next week?

Dialogue 2

A   Paul, do you have a minute?

B   Actually, I'm just on my way to a meeting.

A   Just a second …

B   OK. How can I help?

A   The figures we got from Italy last month don't seem right to me. If you look at page …

B   Sorry, just to clarify, which figures?

A   Sorry, these are gross sales from the Milan office.

B   OK. Go on …

Dialogue 3

A   So, that brings me to the tenth dimension of this problem…

B   Sorry to interrupt again. What was the eighth dimension? I didn't catch that.

A   Number eight was finance. I spoke about profit and loss, remember? I talked you through the budget figures from last year and then gave projections for this coming year.

B   Oh, I thought that was number seven. Look, are there many more points?

page 49

1   Result-oriented

2   People-focused

3   Information-oriented

🎧 TRACK 8

Meeting 1

Anna   So we expect to finish the project on schedule at the end of the month.

Jean-Paul   Excellent. Very good result.

Anna   And in terms of the implementation phase, I expect that …

Jean-Paul   Sorry, when will implementation begin so we actually start to see results?

Anna   Yes, good point. It's the key moment for the project. It will begin on July 1.

Jean-Paul   Right.

Meeting 2

Keith   So that's really all I have to report on the project. Hard work, but I'm happy.

Jean-Paul   Great. Fantastic job. I guess you must be a little tired?

Keith   Absolutely. It was a lot of work.

Jean-Paul   Yes, I'm sure. So how did your family manage with your travel? You were away every week last month.

Keith   Thanks, it was a little difficult but we're OK now it's over. Anyway, how about dinner at the weekend? Now that I have more time.

Jean-Paul   Great. Shall I book somewhere?

Meeting 3

Helen   So that's the report back from the markets. The detailed analysis shows that we're in a strong position but that there are one or two worrying trends which we need to consider in the coming months. The statistics on consumer buying habits at weekends are a little worrying, in fact.

Jean-Paul   What were the statistics exactly?

Helen   If we look at this chart, you'll see some percentages showing a move from buying of brands to buying of own label.

Jean-Paul   I see. And how do you analyse the data?

Helen   Well, for me …

Unit 14   page 51

Roberto clarifies the meaning of *a little*. Later in the conversation he focuses on *my feeling* because he thinks more hard facts are needed – not just feelings – before an important decision can be made.

🎧 TRACK 9

Ian   Yes, so Roberto, what I would like to do in this meeting is focus on pricing. I have the feeling that we may need to reduce our prices a little next year – closer to the level of the competition.

Roberto   Ian, what does 'a little' mean exactly?

Ian   Well, my feeling is that we need to look at around 5%. This would bring our list price to a more realistic market price and might open us up to new customers who at the moment see us as too expensive.

Roberto   OK. You said 'my feeling …' which worries me slightly. I think we need to see hard facts before taking such a big decision. Could you put some numbers together by the end of the week and then we can meet again to discuss?

Unit 15   page 54

Dialogue 1: Clarifying

Dialogue 2: Closing

Dialogue 3: Developing

Dialogue 4: Opening

🎧 TRACK 10

Dialogue 1

Pilar   So, you want to push e-learning next year as a learning methodology. But what for you is e-learning, exactly?

Klaus   For me, it's just the use of technology in learning: computer-based training, blogs, podcasts, and so on.

Pilar   And your feeling is that this will both save money and improve learning effectiveness?

Klaus   Exactly. If we implement e-learning properly, the benefits can be significant.

Pilar   What is 'significant'?

Klaus   OK, well I believe that we can reduce our training budget by around 10%.

Dialogue 2

Pilar   Right. Is there anything else?

Fiona   No, I don't think so. We talked about holiday cover, didn't we?

Pilar   Yes, you have an action plan to discuss with Paul. So will you tell us next week what happens with that discussion?

Fiona   Yes, I'll email you by the end of the week.

Pilar   Good. So maybe we can stop here and I'll see you …

Dialogue 3

Pilar   So, you want to invest more in leadership training for all second line managers. Yes?

Peter   Yes, that's around thirty people.

Pilar   And can you tell me a little bit more about the type of training you want to do?

Peter   I think we should go for the situational leadership model.

Pilar   OK, but were there any other kinds of model we should also think about?

Dialogue 4

Pilar   So, when did you get in?

Marco   At around ten last night. Not too bad.

Pilar   No, not too late. Is it your first time here?

Marco   Yes, first time in St Petersburg. I was in Moscow last year.

Pilar   Moscow? That's another country altogether.

Module four

Unit 16   page 57

(*Target*)

The chairperson, Paul, wants to hear what the meeting participants think about the future reorganisation – its objectives and impact. The participants want to be briefed by senior management. The chairperson should have discussed and clarified the objective of the meeting with the participants personally in advance.

🎧 TRACK 11

Paul   So, let's get started. What I want to do today is to talk a little bit about the new reorganisation, to hear your views on the change objectives and future impact. I think it's important that we all understand what's happening and why. So, can we go quickly around the table and hear views on this? Sonja?

Sonja   But I was expecting you to brief us today about the reorganisation.

Paul   No. The objective for the meeting today is for me to hear your understanding of the changes which are coming and how you see the impacts on your departments.

Steve   I think we need to have a briefing first – to hear what senior management expects before we give our opinion about this.

Paul   I understand that but this is not about senior management telling people what to do, it's about you understanding the need for change and taking responsibility for change.

Sonja   Absolutely not. It's the responsibility of the board to be clear about ...

page 58

(*Information*)

The speaker, Pierre, does not make a very good choice of topic. In fact, hunting is against the personal values of the listener, Jan. In terms of detail, the speaker uses difficult vocabulary like deer which the listener has to clarify.

🎧 TRACK 12

Pierre   Yes, so I go hunting maybe ten times over the summer. Mainly deer and ...

Jan   Sorry, what was that, Pierre?

Pierre   Deer. A big animal in the forest.

Jan   OK, I see.

Pierre   Yeah, and so there are normally around five of us, with dogs. It's great ... to be outdoors, to be with friends and it can be quite exciting to hunt, you against the animal, you know what I mean?

Jan   Mmn, I see what you mean. But I'm a vegetarian. Hunting isn't really my thing so much, but ...

(*Process*)

Klaus makes clear he wants to discuss price again. He explains this as the normal way for him to negotiate. Klaus is successful in that Peter accepts this, even though he feels the question of price is already settled. However, Peter may have been left feeling annoyed.

🎧 TRACK 13

Klaus   So, I would like to start with price as the first part of the negotiation.

Peter   Erm ...

Klaus   I know that you probably think that we've finalised price already and that this is not for negotiation ...

Peter   Yes, I thought it was settled.

Klaus   But I think we need to talk again about this just to be clear before we move on to terms and conditions. For me, this is a typical negotiation process so I hope it is OK for you.

Peter   OK, so just to be clear, you want to summarise as a kind of beginning?

page 59

(*Style*)

John gives information about a serious production problem in a very indirect way. His American colleague, Jim, misunderstands this indirectness – 'a little problem' – until John describes the problem more explicitly. In a way, both are responsible for the misunderstanding; John uses a communication style which confuses his American colleague. However, Jim shows a lack of sensitivity to John's communication style – he should realise that 'a little problem' could be a big problem. John could have avoided the misunderstanding by adapting his communication style and stating the problem more directly.

🎧 TRACK 14

John   Hi, Jim. Look, I need to talk to you about a little problem we have.

Jim   John, sorry but I'm really busy right now. If it's just a little problem, can't it wait until tomorrow?

John   Ah, well, when I said a little problem, I meant ... well ... we have a problem with production. Two lines are down with a technical problem.

Jim   Two lines down? Well, what do you mean, a little problem? This is a disaster.

John   Yes, well, that's what I meant, so ... I think we need to discuss how to ...

Unit 17   page 60

1 In the first phone conversation John thinks that Sabine is criticising him. In the second phone call Sabine communicates more positively by expressing appreciation that John is very busy. She then explains that she needs the information for a presentation to the Board the next morning.

TRACK 15

Call 1

John   John Albrooke.

Sabine   John, it's Sabine. John, I really need the data on the Chinese market which I asked for last week. It's now late. Can you send it today, please?

John   Sabine, sorry but I've been very busy. I just didn't have time.

Sabine   Sorry, John, I wasn't criticising it's just that I really need the data ...

TRACK 16

Call 2

John   John Albrooke.

Sabine   John, it's Sabine. John, I appreciate that you're very busy at the moment but could you send me the Chinese figures I asked for last week? I really need them by the end of the day for a presentation to the Board tomorrow morning. Is that possible?

John   Sure. I'm a little busy but I'll get the information to you as soon as I can. I should be able to ...

2 Not the objective: To present solutions

   Actual objective: To present options and take a decision together

TRACK 17

Sarah   So, let's get started. To begin with, I think it's important to clarify the objective of the presentation today because there may be different understandings of why we're here. What I don't want to do is to present solutions. What I really want to do is talk about options – and then we can discuss the options and make a decision together.

3 Suggestion 1: Slow down

   Suggestion 2: Keep explanations shorter

   Suggestion 3: Write key ideas on a flip chart

TRACK 18

Paul   ... and, to be honest, I think we need to look very seriously at the whole IT infrastructure as I don't think it is really supporting the business – I think the functionality is all wrong – remember the problems we had last year with the Italian data? – absolute nightmare for everyone involved – so we need to think long and hard about ...

Sophie   Paul, sorry to interrupt but I can see that Alexandra is having problems following you – you know she struggles a little bit with your English.

Paul   Sorry, I was off again.

Sophie   Can you slow down, and maybe keep things a little shorter, the long explanations are difficult to follow.

Paul   Sure.

Sophie   And maybe you can write key ideas or words on the flip chart so we have a clear idea of the main points.

page 61

4 Question 1: Is the issue of quality clear?

   Question 2: Is 98% quality OK?

   Point clarified: How to increase quality to 98%

TRACK 19

Dirk   So in terms of our needs, as I said, the most important thing for us is to have the right colour quality in the product, as this is very important for our customers. Is the issue of quality clear?

Simone   Absolutely, and there's no problem there. We can deliver the quality you need.

Dirk   When I mentioned quality, I said that we needed 98%. Is 98% quality OK?

Simone   Sorry, I didn't hear you say that. Normally, we can only guarantee 95%.

Dirk   Right, that's very important. We need to clarify how we can increase the quality to 98% as this is really a must for us.

Unit 19   page 65

Conversation 1: Exclusivity

Conversation 2: Social proof

TRACK 20

Conversation 1

Maria   So, what do you think about the job in Moscow? I think it's a unique opportunity for you to build up a very successful operation there. And the salary is great – much better than is offered for normal postings abroad. And there's the opportunity to live in one of the world's greatest cities. What do you say?

Caroline   It sounds really good. I just have a few questions though.

Conversation 2

Stephan   Ingrid, when are we planning the end-of-project celebration party?

Ingrid   Party? I wasn't planning a party. We finished the project. Now we move on. We don't really do any kind of party in Sweden.

Stephan   Yes, but this is Switzerland. It's very normal around here, part of the culture in a way. I think it would send some mixed messages if we didn't do it. People might even think the project was unsuccessful.

Ingrid   OK, I need to think about this. I didn't realise the culture here. It's good to know. So maybe we could do something at the end of the month …

Module five

Unit 21   page 73

Presentation 1	Presentation 2
1 yes	no
2 yes	no
3 yes	no
4 yes	yes

(*Culture strategy commentary*)

In some contexts such a strategy will work, if enough members of the audience want to be flexible. It's more likely to be successful if the presenter is known to the audience and there is trust. If not, it may be a better strategy for the presenter to adapt.

TRACK 21

Extract 1

So what I want to do today is to go through the new quality processes which we're all planning to implement next month. This is an important briefing and should deliver a clear benefit for all of you, namely, to help you manage the implementation efficiently. In terms of my role, as Head of Quality for the business division, I've engineered this process change, so if there are any questions now or problems later, you should come directly to me. In terms of today, I'd prefer this session to be much more a dialogue with questions and comments, because I need your full understanding and engagement to make this a success. We have a lot to do in the next few weeks and I hope the session today can enable you to go away and do the job of implementation quickly and successfully.

Extract 2

My objective today is to show our new ideas for the brand campaign we're running at the end of the month. Now, John tells me that you're going to have lots of questions and that it's very much the culture in Italy to interrupt and join in. That's fine, but for today as we have so little time, and as I'm not a marketing expert as such, what I'd like to do is to go through everything once – no questions – and then take questions at the end. But again I don't want too much discussion and analysis today – we already have a decision and we need to clarify what we have to do to make the brand campaign a success. OK?

Unit 22   page 74

Step 1: <u>John, do you have any comments? You told me that were a little unsure before I started?</u>

Step 2: <u>You mean the data for the whole project, or the pilot?</u> (*clarify*); <u>OK, it's a good question.</u> (*feedback*)

Step 4: <u>OK?</u>

Step 5: <u>Right, let's now turn to marketing.</u>

TRACK 22

(see page 74)

page 75

Step 1: <u>Are there any questions about this or comments so far?</u>

Step 2: <u>Good. I think that's a critical question because we all need to be very clear about why we're doing this.</u>

Step 4: <u>Can you see that?</u>

Step 5: <u>So, any more questions about complexity or can we move on?</u>

🎧 **TRACK 23**

(see page 75)

page 76

🎧 **TRACK 24**

Audience member   Isn't this going to take a long time to implement? It looks to me almost impossible.

Speaker   That's a good question, but we have to make the impossible possible! As I said, our board has made the decision to do this – whatever the cost and whatever the time – for strategic reasons. The question is not when, but how. This presentation is about how all of us – you, me and the others in this room – can deliver the results our board expects from us. I agree it won't be easy, but let's make the impossible possible together.

Unit 23   page 77

Surface: <u>I know that some of you would like to discuss these problems and the reasons for them in detail</u> …

Satisfy: <u>We'll find time next week to analyse the causes of the problems in more detail</u> …

Suggest: … <u>but I really want this meeting to focus just on what we need to do in the next two weeks to get things back on track a little.</u>

<u>… but I would like to focus on next steps today. Is that OK with everyone?</u>

🎧 **TRACK 25**

(see page 77)

page 78

🎧 **TRACK 26**

Peter   OK, shall we get down to business? You all have the agenda? Yes? Good. I'd like to go through it point by point in the order as written, spending five minutes only on each topic. Remember to bear in mind the rules which we follow for our meetings – follow the agenda, no interruptions, everyone should say something … please say if you disagree, and so on. You all know these rules but I've displayed them again for you on the flipchart. OK? Good. So, Sue, could you start with the first point?

Sue   Right, to begin I'd like to …

Sven   But before we talk about the problem in hand, Peter, I'd like to go back in time to the beginning of the year. If you remember, it was a difficult period.

Peter   Sorry, Sven, remember the rules about following the agenda and interruptions? We've all agreed to these. Let's hear Sue and we can deal with any points when she asks for questions. Sue.

Sue   Thank you. So, as I was saying …

Unit 24   page 80

1 c   2 a   3 b

Dirk may feel a little irritated by Danielle's communication style in the meeting. She is not following the structured approach he prefers and her listening style uses interruption, a behaviour which Dirk may see as impolite and unprofessional.

🎧 **TRACK 27**

Dirk   OK, in my view there are three ways to solve the staffing problem. We could recruit somebody. But this is too expensive. We don't have the money. This means we really need to promote internally. However, we have the problem that there is nobody in the department at the moment who is suitably qualified. So I think we should look at candidates from other departments, and I think there are three options. Firstly, there's Jane from Group Audit. You can see from the documentation I sent you in advance of the meeting that …

Danielle   … Oh, Jane is great. I wonder if the problem really is staffing though. Could we take some time to look at budgets?

Dirk   Danielle, I'd like to finish my summary of the candidates, discuss this and then take a decision. We need to take a decision today about people and not discuss budgets. OK? Good. So, the second possible candidate is from Marketing, a young guy with a lot of potential. Less experienced but I think he has the right mindset.

Per-Erik   You mentioned mindset, Dirk. Do you think this is the critical factor?

Dirk   Yes, I do. At the end of the day, I think we should look at a younger person who has a good attitude, even with less experience. But we need to …

Danielle   I don't agree. I think experience is really important if we want the person to deliver high-quality results. Don't we have someone with more experience?

page 81

TRACK 28

Nicola   I think we need to spend more money on personal development if we want to keep our good people happy.

Serge   OK. I see.

Nicola   Yes, and if we keep good people happy, these people stay in the company. What do you think?

Serge   I think in many ways you're right. So for you, creating a training culture is part of a broader strategy to maintain our talent pool?

Nicola   Exactly.

Serge   My feeling is that the job itself is probably more significant than the training policy, although the latter may be important.

Nicola   Interesting.

Serge   Yes, my feeling is that if people have interesting jobs then they'll stay in the company. So what we have to do is make sure people feel that they are doing something interesting and fulfilling. You see what I mean?

Nicola   Yes, and I can agree …

(Disagreement styles)

It's difficult to say if Hans's communication is effective or ineffective in this specific situation because Riccardo's reaction is not clearly positive or negative – he simply asks for time to think. If Riccardo is happy to hear an honest and open opinion, Hans's directness will be seen positively. If he sees Hans's phrase as a personal attack – not simply a statement about the facts of the case – then he may be feeling angry and react emotionally.

TRACK 29

Hans   I think we need to spend more money on marketing if we want to grow the business. What do you think? Riccardo?

Riccardo   You may be right, Hans, but I'm not sure. I think it could be interesting to invest a little bit more money in new product development.

Hans   No, you're totally wrong. We have the right products but we need to communicate this better to customers.

Riccardo   OK, I hear what you're saying, but can you say why …

Unit 25   page 82

Maria's approach may create difficulties in two ways. Firstly, she could be seen as rather 'pushy' in some cultural contexts where the decision-making process is not forced so quickly and explicitly by the leader of a meeting. It is possible that she is seen as somebody who moves to decisions too quickly without proper consideration of all the data. Secondly, she accepts Mario's 'Yes, OK.' a little too quickly as a sign of agreement. In international contexts 'yes' might not mean 'yes'. People may prefer to say yes rather than admit that they don't fully understand – they think things can be clarified later. People may also be unwilling to say no because they don't want to generate conflict. Therefore, it can be important when leading meetings to do a final check if participants have any final questions or doubts about the decision, e.g. *Before we move to actions, are there any final questions people would like to raise?* or *Will this decision create any problems for you?*

TRACK 30

Maria   We're running a little short of time here. I think we need to take a decision on this. John, you agree with the proposal? Petra too, yes?

Petra   Yes.

Maria   Good. And Mario. Can you go with my idea?

Mario   Yes, OK.

Maria   Good, so we all agree to implement the new software from Telcom by the end of the year. What we need to do now is define roles and responsibilities. Petra, can you handle the discussions with IT and get some feedback from them on possible risks, say by end of the month?

page 83

The missing step is: Arrange a date for the next meeting.

TRACK 31

OK, if there are no further items to discuss … no? … then let me summarise the meeting briefly and clarify next steps. So, the main outcome is that we've agreed to set up a call centre in Bratislava. That was the major objective. And we've also mapped out a project team which will take responsibility for that – Peter as leader and Adriane as deputy. Timeframe for completion is a little open but by end next year at the latest. Is that OK for everyone? Good. Then in terms of actions, the key next step is mine. I need to clarify budget with the sponsor for the project. Once that is done, we can look at defining the project scope and tasks more clearly. That's in the minutes, Jackie, yes? Good. Right, then I'd like to close by saying great job. It's been a difficult meeting in many ways but a great result and I think we really have a good level of commitment to push this process forward. So, let's close there and ... safe trips home. Thanks.

Module six

Unit 26   page 87

(*sample email*)
I would be really grateful if you could send me the results of the employee engagement survey for the Italian business unit by the end of the day. Apologies for such short notice, but I have just had a request to create a report for the board so am also under a lot of pressure. I really appreciate your support with this.

Unit 27   page 88

(*Building rapport*)

Call 1

Sam starts the call by asking a number of polite questions both personal – *How are you doing?*, *And family?* – and about work – *How about with you? Are you busy?*– which show interest in Andrew and create time for relationship-building.

Call 2

Sam uses the phrase *Right, I'm calling to* ... to introduce the business topic.

TRACK 32

Call 1

Andrew   Hello, Andrew speaking.
Sam   Andrew, hi. It's Sam. How are you doing?
Andrew   Good, and you?
Sam   I'm OK, just about. Lot of work on at the moment. How about with you? Are you busy?
Andrew   It's not too bad. Quite a lot of work from our Indian customers at the moment.
Sam   Great. And family?
Andrew   Very well, thank you. And for you too, I hope?
Sam   Absolutely. In fact, yesterday ...

Call 2

Victor   Hello? Victor Nazarov.
Sam   Victor, Sam calling.
Victor   Morning, Sam.
Sam   Right, I'm calling to finalise logistics for the workshop next week. You have time now?
Victor   Sure.
Sam   OK, we need to agree ...

(*Clear communication*)
Sam asks two important questions: firstly to clarify meaning – What do you mean by 'difficult'? – and secondly to clarify needs – What do you need exactly?

TRACK 33

Mary   Mary Conway.
Sam   Hi, Mary. Sam calling.
Mary   Hi, Sam. You need to be quick. Just on my way to a meeting. Sorry.
Sam   No problem. I just need you to confirm when I'll have your project report. Your email didn't actually specify that.
Mary   Yeah, as I said in the email, things are kind of difficult with that.
Sam   What do you mean by 'difficult'?
Mary   Well, we've got two guys off sick at the moment so progress has been sort of slow this month. So not really a lot to report.
Sam   OK. You also said in your email you were waiting for information from Purchasing? What do you need exactly?
Mary   We just need clarification on when ...

(*Extra information*)
Sam asks two general questions to discover interesting news in the supplier's company: ... *and how are things generally in the company?* and *Any interesting developments?*

TRACK 34

Sam   So when can we expect delivery, Jan?
Jan   We'll be able to deliver by the end of the month.
Sam   Great ... and yeah, how are things generally in the company? Any interesting developments?
Jan   Yes, well you maybe heard that we're thinking of outsourcing the actual delivery side of the business. That could be good for you because it'll probably mean lower costs and faster service.

page 89

(Prevent conflict)

Sam uses two strategies when she hears John's misunderstanding of her question. Firstly, she explicitly says what she didn't mean: 'Sorry, no, John, I wasn't criticising you or the team', and then she explicitly explains the positive intention behind her message: 'I'm just asking you personally now, because I know I can rely on you to get me the most up-to-date information before the meeting which is really important.' This clarification and clear statement of positive intention enables the communication to move forward positively.

🎧 TRACK 35

Sam   John, the data your team sent me last week on the project wasn't correct. Can you look at it personally and send me the correct figures by the end of today? I have a meeting with the project leader later.

John   Hey, everyone is complaining and, you know, it wasn't my fault. We had an IT problem which corrupted the figures …

Sam   Sorry, no, John, I wasn't criticising you or the team. Absolutely not. I know there was a technical problem. I'm just asking you personally now, because I can rely on you to get me the up-to-date information before the meeting which is really important.

John   OK, I see. Well, yes, no problem. Yes, I can do that, in a couple of hours?

Sam   Great.

Unit 28   page 90

(The beginning)

Do you know each other?

Can you say a few words about yourself as a quick introduction?

🎧 TRACK 36

Automatic voice   Patrick has entered the meeting.

Chair   Hi, Patrick. Bob here. Welcome to the meeting.

Patrick   Hi.

Automatic voice   Sandra has entered the meeting.

Chair   Hi, Sandra.

Sandra   Hi, Bob.

Chair   Sandra, Patrick from Ireland is here. Do you know each other?

Sandra   No. Hi, Patrick.

Patrick   Hi, Sandra. Nice to meet you.

Chair   Sandra, Patrick will be your contact point in the Irish office. Can you say a few words about yourself as a quick introduction?

Sandra   Sure. So, I've been working in Chicago now for …

page 91

(Starting well)

The chair doesn't propose the guideline 'Participants should express agreement verbally'. It's a meeting with many participants, so it's easier to use silence to indicate agreement. If anyone disagrees, then they should speak out.

🎧 TRACK 37

Chair   OK, can we start with some ground rules for the meeting? Because there are a lot of new people here I would propose we introduce ourselves by name before we speak. And if you have a question for someone, can you address them by name too. It just makes things clearer. I'll interrupt from time to time just to keep things on track. So don't take that personally. And please only speak if you have a point to make, or if you don't understand or you disagree with something. We can take silence as agreement. We don't need to waste time saying I agree and things like this. OK?

page 92

(Listening effectively)

João interrupts the chair to deal with the issue immediately. Maria waits patiently until the chair invites questions and then goes back to the point of an earlier misunderstanding.

🎧 TRACK 38

Extract 1

Chair   So what I propose to do now is …

João   Sorry, but may I interrupt?

Chair   Erm, OK. João, yes?

João   I have a question …

Extract 2

Chair   … we're deciding to postpone the launch of the PX35 until next year. Of course, this will bring a few problems for all of us, but I think we all agree it's better to launch when the product is right rather than simply to keep to the schedule. OK, are there any questions at this stage?

Maria   Yes, one question.

Chair   Maria, go on.

Maria   You were talking five minutes ago about technical problems. Can we discuss this again, as I think there may be a misunderstanding?

(*Speaking effectively*)
What happens if we don't invest now? Derek uses this type of question to highlight the urgency of immediate investment. Importantly, he almost certainly knows how John will answer and how it will support his argument.

TRACK 39

Derek   So, for me the production problem was actually good news. It showed us we have some serious health and safety issues which we need to manage in order to improve conditions for our staff. The major issue now is investment. I feel we have to invest urgently, even if times are difficult, to make the production area 110% safe. John, you've done the safety audit. What happens if we don't invest now?

John   I think it's very likely that because we've waited so long that …

Unit 29   page 95

Speaker 1: Issues and priorities for negotiation
The seller believed price was a critical issue for discussion in the negotiation. The buyer wanted to concentrate on other factors, like delivery.

Speaker 2: Basic concept of negotiation / Agreement and legal contract
The partners probably saw the negotiation more as a getting-to-know process, where the discussion was not to reach agreement quickly, but simply to build a relationship and explore the potential for agreement. The speaker, who was very goal-oriented, may have misinterpreted the discussion as indicating agreement when in fact the partners were only agreeing with the possibility of agreement.

Speaker 3: Communication style / Issues and priorities for negotiation
In this anecdote the speaker describes his confusion with the communication style of his counterpart, which seemed very unstructured. His eventual success was because he identified a priority issue or need for his counterpart – making contacts with important people in society – and was able to make an offer to satisfy this need.

TRACK 40

Speaker 1   I had some problems negotiating with a couple of companies which I was trying to sell to. It was very difficult to discuss price with them. Normally, as a supplier, I would start with a high price and then negotiate down a little closer to the buyer position. But with these companies, the first price given to me was the final price. I found it really frustrating, to be honest, and so we discussed it over lunch. The buyer explained by saying that in his culture not negotiating price was a kind of honesty. It was like they didn't want to give me a false price at the beginning, so they started with the final price, which was non-negotiable. The actual negotiation was around other things like delivery, quality and so on, not price. When I understood this I felt a lot better.

Speaker 2   I couldn't believe it. We had a two-day negotiation with our partners. Eventually, we got a verbal agreement to go with the deal. But when I emailed over a paper contract, I got a reply back saying that we hadn't agreed anything at the meeting. In fact, the guy seemed to be saying that we hadn't even discussed a couple of the key issues at all. For me, this wasn't intercultural misunderstanding. It was purely tactical and, from my point of view, totally unacceptable. In the end I didn't reply to the email and just walked away from the deal.

Speaker 3   I was having real problems selling our solution to the client. It was taking forever and was quite confusing – there were so many people in the room and involved, sometimes I didn't know who I was meant to be negotiating with. Anyway, I'd read that contacts were important in this country and so, because I knew people at the embassy, I said to my counterpart that if he signed, I might be able to set up a meeting for him with a member of the royal family. So I was offering this guy something special. You won't believe how quickly he signed. And that's a tip for international negotiating: know the culture and use the right cultural tools which will get you to an agreement.

Unit 30   page 96

(*Test your intercultural sensitivity*)

Extract 1: Use a middleman

Extract 2: Improvise

Extract 3: Do it their way

 TRACK 41

Extract 1

John   OK, before we begin, shall we just do a few introductions? I'd like to welcome Alexander, who you won't have met before. I've asked him to join us as he's a Russian speaker, and so he can help you with any language issues. He's also very experienced in both Russia and Canada in this form of negotiation so I'm hoping he will act as a kind of cultural bridge to support us.

Extract 2

John   So, how shall we proceed today?

Customer 1   I think we can just get started. I don't think we need a formal process. We know each other pretty well, so let's just begin with what we think is important and we can look to structure things a little later if necessary.

John   Sounds fine to me.

Extract 3

John   So, it's great to be back. I think this is visit number 35 to Argentina. It's beginning to feel a little like home.

Customer 2   Well, you are most welcome, as always. So, how shall we proceed?

John   I'm happy to follow you. I think I know how you like to do things and I'm happy to go with that today.

Customer 2   Great. So then, as you know, we always like to start with a little review of the market situation.

page 97

(*Negotiating how to negotiate*)

Step 1: <u>Before we start, I think it would be useful to clarify a little how we plan to negotiate today.</u>

Step 2: <u>One of the main issues is how we see our roles. From our side, we have a lot of scope to discuss all the issues, but in terms of any final agreement we have to go back to our senior management for approval.</u>

Step 3: <u>That means for us we should see this part of the negotiation as a first discussion phase and we would be looking to finalise things at another meeting at some point in the future. How does that sound?</u>

Step 4: <u>No, that's fine from our point of view. I think we have scope to agree to a 90% solution which we can move to a deal by the end of the month?</u>

 TRACK 42

(see page 97)

Module seven

Unit 32   page 103

Meeting 1

Is this your first time in Ghana?
In Accra?
So you know a little of my wonderful city.
Can I get you something to drink?

Meeting 2

So, you had a good trip? No problems?
Something to drink before we start?

It's not easy to say which conversation is more successful. In fact, Kwame handles both conversations successfully but uses a different style in each. In the first, he asks more questions, as Mary seems to be enthusiastic and happy to spend time in small talk. In the second conversation, he asks fewer questions and moves more quickly to business in response to Sabine's shorter answers and her willingness to get started on business. The way she says So suggests she is keen to end the small talk phase. See Building rapport in Unit 33.

 TRACK 43

Meeting 1

Kwame   Mary?

Mary   That's right. Nice to meet you. Only a voice on the phone till now.

Kwame   That's right. Nice to meet you too. Welcome to Ghana.

Mary   Thank you. It's good to be here.

Kwame   Is this your first time in Ghana?

Mary   No, actually second. I was here for a conference last year.

Kwame   Oh, really. In Accra?

Mary   Yes, at the Hyatt.

Kwame   So you know a little of my wonderful city.

Mary   Well, I didn't see a great deal last time, mainly just hotel walls.

Kwame   OK, well we'll have to arrange a little tour for you during your stay. Now, please, take a seat. Can I get you something to drink?

Mary   Great, could I have …

Meeting 2

Kwame   Sabine?

Sabine   Yes.

Kwame   OK, nice to meet you. Please take a seat.

Sabine   Thank you.

Kwame   So, you had a good trip? No problems?

Sabine   Yes, thank you. Fine.

Kwame   OK. Good. Something to drink before we start?

Sabine   No, thanks. I had coffee at breakfast. So …

Kwame   OK, then I think we can get started. The agenda today is …

Unit 33   page 106

Jean is more the coconut (more reserved, shorter answers to questions, less personal information) with Alex more the peach (more talkative, more focus on personal life, asking more questions).

Javier's general rapport-building strategy is to adapt his approach to the style and expectations of the other person. In both situations, however, he tries to engage people in conversation by using questions. In the first conversation, Javier concentrates more on facts and professional topics, for example *And what's his main area of expertise?*. In the second, he focuses quickly on feelings and personal life outside work, for example *What've you been up to? Anything exciting?* He uses a more openly enthusiastic tone of voice and positive vocabulary than in the first conversation where the general tone is more neutral.

TRACK 44

Conversation 1

Javier   So, how are you today, Jean?

Jean   Good.

Javier   Busy?

Jean   As usual, yes.

Javier   How did the meeting go today?

Jean   Very good. As usual, a lot of talking but we got some good decisions on the project.

(*Pause*)

Javier   Next week I have a meeting with Paul Smith from the UK to discuss the common finance policy. You know him, I think.

Jean   Yes, a little.

Javier   And what's his main area of expertise?

Jean   Oh, he's very good. He has a strong knowledge of European law and he knows a lot about …

Conversation 2

Javier   So, how's life, Alex?

Alex   Good. How about you?

Javier   I'm good. A bit tired after the weekend.

Alex   Really? What've you been up to? Anything exciting?

Javier   Yeah, well we had some friends round on Saturday evening, old friends from university. It was really good to catch up. What about you? Weren't you going to Paris?

Alex   That was the plan but Helen was ill so we decided to postpone things to …

Unit 34   page 107

Phase 1: So, are you going back to Mexico for summer?

Phase 2: Two open questions: How long are you going for then? Where will you stay?

Phase 3: They both have friends living in Austin, Texas.

TRACK 45

Ben   So, how's it going?

Alejandro   Good. And you?

Ben   Yeah, very good.

(*slight pause*)

Ben   So, are you going back to Mexico for the summer?

Alejandro   Yeah. And I'm taking a long holiday this year. Gives me a chance to meet all the family and friends. A lot of people to see.

Ben   How long are you going for then?

Alejandro   Three weeks.

Ben   Wow! Great! Where will you stay?

Alejandro   Well, we still have a small apartment in Cancun, so there most of the time, but we'll also do a bit of travelling in the south of Texas. I have a couple of old college friends living there.

Ben   Texas? I have some friends living in Texas, in Austin.

Alejandro   Yeah, that's where my friends are, downtown Austin. Maybe they know each other.

Ben   Yeah, maybe.

Unit 35   page 108

(*'push' / 'pull' styles*)
The first conversation demonstrates the 'push' style, the second the 'pull' style.

'Pull' questions: What should we do? Could we find a middle way? What do you think? Could you discuss it with him today?

🎧 TRACK 46
Conversation 1

Luis   Look, I think we need to discuss this problem with John as soon as possible.

Javed   I'm not sure. You know his approach – he expects us to solve any problems. Only go to him if we have solutions.

Luis   Yeah, I know that, but this is serious. I think we need to inform him now rather than wait and test out our own solutions.

Javed   I'm not sure, but if you insist.

Luis   Good. OK. I'll call him later and tell him we would like a meeting to discuss things as soon as possible.

Javed   OK. Fine.

Conversation 2

Luis   So, Petra, we have a problem with the schedule. What should we do?

Petra   I think we need to postpone the launch. The logistics are simply not in place. It's not good because we'll have to inform the board of the delay.

Luis   OK. Could we find a middle way? We keep the launch date but launch in only a few markets. This means we don't have to go back to the board and inform them of a problem. What do you think?

Petra   Yes, but I'm not sure John will agree.

Luis   Could you discuss it with him today?

Petra   Yes, I can do that in the team meeting later. OK, let's see what he says.

page 109

(*Be transparent*)
Helena states explicitly her intention is to listen and her intention is not to implement a programme which people disagree with.

🎧 TRACK 47

Helena   OK, the objective of the presentation today is to tell you where we are with the talent management initiative, which I'm sure many of you have heard about. Before I start, I think it's important to clarify a couple of things to avoid any misunderstanding. Firstly, I know that many of you are unsure about this idea. You feel that picking some people out as so-called *talents* sends very negative and demotivating messages to non-talents. This is something we totally agree with you about, and so we need to agree a process which avoids this. Let me say very clearly that our intention is very much to listen to your ideas before we make a decision. This is fundamental. So the ideas I will present today are very much work in progress and something we should discuss more together. Our intention is not to implement a talent management programme which you disagree with. We want something which you want to have.

page 110

(*Be strong*)
Jacob uses strong language: *I think it would be crazy ...*
He states personal conviction explicitly: *I really believe ...*
He refers clearly to negative consequences of inaction: *If we don't, I think we risk ...*

🎧 TRACK 48

Jacob   Look, I think it would be crazy to hold the next meeting in Zurich again. I really believe we need to rotate meetings around the European business units. If we don't, I think we risk sending the wrong messages about the company being centralised in Switzerland, run by the Swiss for the Swiss ... and, in the end, we'll lose the commitment from the smaller companies for the project.

page 111

(*Be prepared*)
The people using the computers are the problem. They are downloading too much data on to their local computers causing them to run slowly.

🎧 TRACK 49

Jason   My feeling is that we need to use the budget next year to invest in better IT equipment. The computers are really slow – it means we're wasting time and that's causing a lot of irritation.

Anton   The problem is not the computers, it's the people using them. If you look at these stats I prepared, it shows how much personal data people have downloaded from the internet on to their computers. This is putting pressure on memory and slowing the computers down.

Jason   But the computers don't have enough memory in the first place. They need more just to run the operating system.

Anton   I checked that too with people in our IT department. They said the computers had enough memory. The problem is data overload.

Chair   OK, well it seems we need to deal with this issue of data download urgently. How should we proceed? Any ideas?

Module eight

Unit 36   page 113

John Hansen: responsibilities within the team, knowledge and skills you have which are relevant for the team's tasks, experience of working in international teams, positive expectations about working in the team

Jim Chambers: responsibilities within the team, knowledge and skills you have which are relevant for the team's tasks, experience of working in international teams, background personal information, positive expectations about working in the team

TRACK 50

John Hansen   OK, so let me kick off the introductions as head of the project. Where to start? Well, my background is in fact in consultancy and training, I spent a couple of years in the US as a leadership consultant before joining Bonn Homme in 1981. I was Head of Learning and Development in the Danish company for a year, then Head of HR, and then moved to head of HR in the US around five years ago. As for my interests and skills, these are very much in leadership. I worked in the US for some time and that experience tells me that the organisation needs a new European Academy which can push its leadership capability forward into the future. So I'm very happy to be leading this project – my first European project – and I'm looking forward to working with you all to deliver something very important for our organisation. OK, Jim.

Jim Chambers   Thanks, John. OK, so I'm Jim Chambers. I head up the Learning and Development activities we have in Chicago, and coordinate things across our US offices. My task in the project is to be John's deputy, and to support him with the benefit of the experiences we had when we set up our US Academy three years ago.

I heard that John is new to the European project game. Well, this will be my fifth major European project so I really hope I can bring some of that experience into the team to help us reach our goals. On the personal front, I'm married, two kids and one on the way. So sometime in September don't be surprised if I stop answering emails as I may be in the hospital watching my second son be born. OK, Samantha?

page 114

Samantha focuses on experience and positive expectations.

TRACK 51

Samantha   So, how are you? Enjoying the meeting?

Anshuman   Yeah, it's good to learn about the project and to meet everyone.

Samantha   So, you said in your introduction that you've worked quite a lot in these kinds of projects.

Anshuman   Yes, this is really my background, supporting global projects with IT solutions.

Samantha   You worked in the States a little bit?

Anshuman   Yeah. Of course, I started in India but moved to the US quite soon because that's where the client was usually based, and now here in Europe for a few years.

Samantha   Interesting. And what's your feeling about this project? Any problems you see with it?

Anshuman   No. I mean, it's complex and it won't be easy but I think the team is good, the goal is pretty clear so we just need to make sure we have enough resources. But I'm very positive.

page 115

Samantha is not clear how the new Academy will deliver better quality leadership training. Jim tries to build her commitment by stressing the benefits to the local Spanish organisation and the group as a whole.

TRACK 52

Jim   So, Samantha, did the session this morning on goals help?

Samantha   Yes and no, to be honest. I heard the major goals ... to be more efficient, to deliver higher quality training across Europe, but we have our own leadership training, and we're happy with that and I just don't see how this Academy can deliver a better quality than we have at present. So I'm a little unsure about the project.

Jim   Yes, but it's not only about quality, the project is about creating a common approach to leadership across the group, one leadership mindset for the whole company.

Samantha   OK.

Jim   I think we have to focus on global benefits. All the local business units will benefit from this project if there is a common leadership model established. Common leadership will mean clearer direction, better collaboration, more sharing of ideas, and so on. This has to be a win situation for the UK.

Samantha   OK, this makes sense.

Unit 37   page 116

(*Understanding the sources of conflict*)

The main sources of conflict are *organisation* (Andy cannot access data in his business unit in same way that Nathalie can in hers) and *communication* (neither person is listening very well to the other but rather defending their own position).

🔊 TRACK 53

Nathalie   So when can you deliver the data?

Andy   Nathalie, sorry, but I can't deliver the data you need. I just don't have it.

Nathalie   You must have it. It's basic financial data. I just need totals for all the money spent by the different departments on training last year. What's difficult about that?

Andy   I understand what you want. You were very clear in your email which, by the way, wasn't necessary to copy to John. It really doesn't help involving my boss. As I said, we do the accounting in a different way here so we can't collect these figures. I want to help but I can't.

Nathalie   Look, I have to deliver the figures to my board member by this afternoon. If you can't help me, I'll have to mention this to John again.

Andy   OK, do it. I don't think we can solve this.

(*Preventing conflict*)

Alena suggests having a regular item on the agenda at project team meetings called *Creativity* which will enable the team to discuss any conflict and find creative solutions.

🔊 TRACK 54

Alena   OK, just before we get down to the first presentation, I want to pick up on something that was said earlier about the issue of conflict. You all

know that this project is not, and will not be, easy at times so I think we need to somehow expect and plan for conflict or, let's say, differences of opinion. And remember, we need differences of opinion, we need to listen to each other and use different ideas to find creative solutions. So what I suggest is that in the first six months of the project we have as a regular item on the agenda an item which I would call *Creativity*, which gives everyone the chance to discuss any conflicts or differences about the project and to use these differences of opinion to find new creative solutions for the project. Jan, what do you think?

page 117

The problem person is a native speaker, Peter, who speaks too quickly and uses idiomatic language, both of which make it very difficult for non-native speakers of English to understand him.

🔊 TRACK 55

Peter   So what we need to do is recruit another couple of IT boffins for the project team with the relevant IT expertise. They can give us a hand …

Simone   Sorry, boff…

Peter   Boffin, erm … it means expert.

Simone   OK, I understand.

Peter   … and then once we're back on track and sailing in the right direction …

Simone   Selling?

Peter   Not selling, sailing … erm …

Chair   Look, Peter, perhaps I can summarise. You want to recruit some IT people for the team. We need support, yes?

Peter   Yeah, exactly and …

Chair   Sorry to interrupt, but I think it's difficult for people to follow you at the moment – you know the language problem, you're a little fast for us. Could you put this proposal in an email after the meeting and then we can discuss it at the conference call we have on Friday? OK?

Peter   OK. Fine. Sorry everybody.

Unit 38   page 119

The solution is for Xiang to go to the UK for three rather six months. The two individuals do not explore a range of solutions by asking each other for ideas. In fact, Paula simply makes a proposal and Xiang accepts. This works in this situation but across cultures the team member may accept because he / she believes that it is necessary to accept the manager's solution rather than because he / she agrees. This could lead to problems again in the future.

🎧 TRACK 56

Paula   So, let's get started. Firstly, thanks for all the information you sent regarding this project in the UK. I think I have a better understanding now of why it interests you and why you're applying for the job. And I think we can find a solution, although we need to talk things through a little.

Xiang   OK, good.

Paula   For you, the project will mean you can learn some new technical skills and improve the language. Right?

Xiang   Yes, but I think I can do more than that and really support the UK organisation with my financial knowledge to manage its current problems. That's why I got a little frustrated last week when you were focusing on learning English as the main objective.

Paula   OK, I hear that upset you and I'm sorry about that. OK, well the good news is that I think you can go, but we need a compromise on timing – you know that I have a resource problem here, so I propose to let you go for three not six months, and there is an option to go back next year if things go well.

Xiang   I think six months would be the better solution but I think it's fair.

Paula   Good. Excellent. So we have a result. Thank you. This enables me to talk to Human Resources tomorrow …

Unit 39   page 120

Ann sees her role to serve the customer with products the customer wants. Mary argues that her role is to sell products which the company is able to develop profitably, and to explain to customers clearly when the company is unable to meet their demands.

This form of disagreement is very typical between the people in the Marketing and R & D (Research and Development) departments of large companies. It is a clash of professional rather than country cultures. Marketing people are always very focused on meeting customer demands. R & D people focus more on defining which products it is technically possible to develop at a good profit for the company.

Both individuals are more interested in stating and defending their positions. Unless they begin listening to each other, and negotiate a compromise, this disagreement could escalate into conflict.

🎧 TRACK 57

Ann   Look, my role in marketing is to listen to what our customers need and deliver products to meet those needs. What we've developed so far doesn't do that.

Mary   I understand what you're saying and that for you the customer is very important. But your role for me is to sell to customers what we can develop. We simply can't meet every customer demand – sometimes it's not possible technically, sometimes it's too expensive.

Ann   That's what R&D always says.

Mary   Yes, but it's true and you have to be realistic with customers and not just promise them everything they want.

Ann   I don't think you understand marketing and working with customers. You can't work with customers in this way … tell them that they're wrong … we can't deliver.

Mary   Ann, but you have to understand …

page 121

Jane is unhappy because she sees it as her responsibility to create meeting agendas, not Ann's. Jane asks Ann to discuss ideas for meetings with her personally so that she can decide if the idea should be discussed by everyone at the team meeting.

🎧 TRACK 58

Ann   Ann Sullivan.

Jane   Ann, It's Jane.

Ann   Hi, Jane. I just sent you an email.

Jane   Yes, I got it. That's why I'm calling. A couple of things. Firstly, I'm glad that you and Mary are now talking more constructively about things. We need people in the team to work together, rather than against each other.

Ann   Yes, I think we have a much better understanding. And so we can now go forward in our meetings more constructively.

Jane   Yes, that's an issue we should discuss. As leader of the project it's *my* responsibility to create an agenda for project meetings. These agendas have to be acceptable to our sponsor and steering committee, and it's my role to make sure this happens, not the team members'.

Ann   OK.

Jane   Yes, so I appreciate your enthusiasm in putting this agenda together but we have to agree that this is something I do, it's my responsibility and that in future if you have good ideas, you come to me and I will decide.

Ann   Yes, fine. Sorry, we just wanted ...

Unit 40   page 122

(*Listen to each other*)

Who's your boss? | Why is he against our project?
Julika discovers that Chris's boss is against the project, which is creating pressure for Chris, which in turn reduces his performance in the project.

TRACK 59

Julika   So, Chris, how are you finding the project?

Chris   It's good, but a lot of work. And I still have some problems with my boss back home. He's not very happy for me to work in the project. He says he needs me to concentrate on problems we have in our own business unit.

Julika   Who's your boss?

Chris   Sam Lyons. Do you know him?

Julika   I've heard the name. Why is he against our project?

Chris   I don't think he really agrees with the idea to standardise IT. He's happy with his local solution.

Julika   Really? I didn't realise. No wonder you're so quiet in meetings if you're under this kind of pressure. Shall we talk to Peter about this, because we need to do something.

Chris   Maybe. If Peter could talk to him ...

(*Make it easy for people to communicate*)
Julika asks the native English speakers to wait until the non-native English speakers have given their opinions.

TRACK 60

Julika   OK, shall we start with the first point, the risk report.

Peter   Do you want me to say something about this in terms of background?

Julika   Thanks, Peter, but I'd like to give people a chance to give some first comments before your input. And John, Peter and Kevin, I'll come to you at the end. I just want to give the non-native speakers a chance to speak before the native speakers, just to make sure we get everyone's thoughts on this. OK?

All   Yes. Fine.

page 123

(*Get people to think creatively together*)

Who's an expert on risk here? Daniel? Peter?

TRACK 61

Julika   Christina, what are your thoughts on the risk document?

Christina   Yes, very interesting. In fact, I was wondering if it might be an idea to have someone from the Risk Department attend one of our meetings to give us more expert input. There seem to be some important risks to the project but I'm not sure if we have identified the right actions.

Daniel   I don't think we need anyone from the Risk Department. They don't know the project and, to be honest, this is quite sensitive information.

Peter   I agree. This is our project and I think it gets confused if we use externals like this.

Julika   Who's an expert on risk here? Daniel? Peter?

(*Silence*)

Julika   Exactly. That's why we should perhaps give a little more thought to Christina's idea. Daniel, wouldn't it be useful to get some expert input on some of the risk areas we have?

Daniel   Well, maybe some comment would be useful ...

(*Connect the best ideas together and take a decision*)
Report nothing (do not inform the customer of the delay)
Increase hours of work on the project to minimise the length of the delay

TRACK 62

Bob   So what do you think we should do about the delay? It's really bad news.

Julie   I'm not sure. I guess we need to inform the customer and say we'll put in extra hours to minimise the length of the delay.

James   Yes, but things get really difficult then. They won't be happy. Customers here are very demanding, you know.

Bob   So what do you suggest?

James   Well, I liked your idea. Just do nothing.

Bob   OK, you mean report nothing. But still increase working hours on the project to minimise the delay?

James   Yeah. It could be we can save time later which brings us back on track before the next report goes out to the customer. So why create problems at this stage?

Bob   OK, I can live with that. So go with this idea and report nothing but, like Julie said, increase hours on the project ...

Module nine

Unit 41   page 126

1 Delegating

2 Coaching

3 Directing

4 Supporting

 TRACK 63

1

Leader   How's it going?

Staff member   Good. Everything is just about on schedule. I have to prepare for the appraisal interviews next month and take a look at which people in my team I can recommend for the talent pool. I think you're one of the talent pool sponsors?

Leader   That's right. Let me know if you need any information on the criteria for the nomination or the talent pool process.

Staff member   OK. I think I've got all the information I need, but I'll contact you if I have any questions.

Leader   Great. OK, see you later.

2

Leader   Hi, Carlos. How are the recruitment interviews going? Found anyone for your team yet?

Staff member   It's going well. I've interviewed five people and two are quite interesting, so I plan to invite these back for a second interview.

Leader   Very good. Actually, I'd quite like to sit down with you and talk through the candidates, then sit in on the interviews. Do you have any plans on how to run them – with everyone together like an assessment centre, or more one-to-one interviews?

Staff member   I need to think about this a little more. Can I get back to you with some ideas next week?

3

Leader   Maria, can you let me have a status report for your two projects by the end of the week please? I need to make a report to the Board for next Tuesday.

Staff member   OK.

Leader   And can you make sure you've agreed a training plan with all your staff before 3 October so that I can submit expenditure figures to Finance. Remember that English language skills are a priority with all these international projects, so please check people's levels and talk to HR about getting a teacher for those who need lessons. OK?

Staff member   Right.

4

Leader   How's the presentation for the management workshop coming along? Finished?

Staff member   It's going OK but it's a lot of work. Presentations aren't really my thing but I've got most of the ideas together. I just need to develop a few slides with the sales data now.

Leader   You'll be fine. You did a great job last year if you remember. I think just do what you did in Milan – keep it short, focus very much on success stories from last year and the top three issues for next year.

Staff member   Yeah, that's what I'm trying to do.

Leader   Great. You'll be fine. You're very good in these workshops and promote our work very well to the Board. Maybe talk to Frank about the issues for next year as he may have some useful figures which will help.

Staff member   Great. Thanks. I was planning to do that but I'll give him a call later this morning.

Unit 42   page 127

(*Demand and deliver high standards*)

He promised and got three new people for the project.

 TRACK 64

Team leader   Look, I know that I'm asking a lot of everyone at the moment to do all this overtime. But, remember, I promised that I would get extra staff into the project last year and we got three new people. And they made a huge difference for all of us in sharing the workload. But, unfortunately, we'll have to wait until next month for more people, which is why I need your support at the moment.

page 128

(*Focus on values*)

She stresses honesty.

 TRACK 65

Project leader   I would like to start this presentation by personally declaring my full commitment to this international innovation project. I would like all of you to know that I will support you and this project 110% … and for those of you who don't know me, you'll soon learn that I always deliver on my promises. One of our company's core values is honesty and I want to be honest with you today. This project will not be easy. In fact, there will be many challenges. But with support – my support to you and your support to me – I'm very confident we can be successful.

(*Show people how they can support the vision*)
He says it supports growth.

TRACK 66
International project leader   This project is going to allow the whole organisation to operate with a single IT financial software platform across every business unit worldwide. This will deliver two things: firstly, enormous cost savings and, secondly, much greater transparency on cost figures, meaning we'll be able to steer the business better and deliver more sustainable growth. So your work is directly supporting our main corporate strategy – growth. Your day-to-day work in the office is helping to drive this organisation towards the future. You're really going to make a difference with this project.

(*Stress common responsibility*)
She sees the team as leader.

TRACK 67
Project leader   For this project to be successful I think we need to understand and agree how leadership has to work. My main role is to see that the project is finished on time and on budget. I'm here to coordinate and to take important decisions when decisions need to be taken. But I'm not here to supervise and control you at all times. I'm not here to solve all your problems. I won't be around to answer all of your questions. I want you as a team to take responsibility for the project work, to feel it is your project and to collaborate as a team to find solutions together and to report these solutions to me. If you do need to talk to me about something important, pick up a phone or knock on my door, and I will be there. But I want you all to be leaders of this project, not just me. I need you as a team to become the leader of this project and drive it to success.

Unit 43   page 130

Smaller customers are a little unhappy because they feel the conference was organised to meet the interests of larger customers. Peter is very happy with the feedback.

TRACK 68
Team leader   OK, Peter. To close, just one bit of feedback from the sales conference last week for our customers. Generally, very good, so great job. However, one or two participants thought that the guest speakers were a little weak, not very interesting. And one or two commented that the conference seemed to be organised to meet the needs of the larger customers rather than the smaller ones. So I don't know what you feel about this.
Peter   OK, on the speakers, I agree. On paper they looked good, but they perhaps weren't the right people. I probably should have talked more to them in advance … so I will next time.
Team leader   Good.
Peter   On the big customers point, I'm not sure I agree. I thought I made quite an effort to involve new contacts.
Team leader   Mmn, the issue is that the smaller customers felt you didn't.
Peter   OK, I agree that's important – what the customers felt.
Team leader   Anything you can do differently next time?
Peter   Probably I need to manage the two groups in a more systematic way and maybe create specific mini-events so that both feel properly taken care of. I need to think about it.
Team leader   Good. So that's it. Was it useful feedback?
Peter   Yes, very. I mean I need to know what customers think, so I'm very open to feedback. No problem.

Unit 44   page 131

(Define the objective)

Objective: How to work with an American colleague.

Open question: *Could you tell me a little bit more about the situation?*

🔊 TRACK 69

Coach   OK, shall we get started then? So what would you like to talk about today? Shall we stay with the issue of time management? This was the performance issue we talked about last week. But I'm happy to go with whatever you want.

Coachee   Well, the time management thing is partly connected to a problem or challenge that I'm having with John in the US. As you know, we have to collaborate and exchange best practice but it's not really working. He's asking for too much data which is taking too much time for me to collect … and he doesn't really listen when I explain this … so this could be something. To discuss how to handle him.

Coach   OK. If that's useful for you. Could you tell me a little bit more about the situation?

(Reflect on causes and possible solutions)

Cause: The boss of the American colleague

Open question: *So what's the next step?*

🔊 TRACK 70

Coach   So why is this a problem for you?

Coachee   As I said, he just asks for so much information from me. You know, this isn't a project. The idea was just to exchange information informally for a couple of months.

Coach   So, why is he doing this, do you think?

Coachee   Good question. I think it could be that he's under pressure from his boss, who is very, very demanding – so John probably feels he has to deliver something special. I think that's the reason. So it's probably not him, it's his boss that's the problem in a way.

Coach   So what's the next step?

Coachee   I guess it's about communication and I just need to telephone and talk it through so that we don't keep on having this problem.

page 132

(Initiate a plan)

The coach's questions make the coachee decide on a more concrete plan of when he will contact John. The questions make the coachee realise that better planning is part of improving time management, the larger coaching question mentioned at the beginning of the session.

🔊 TRACK 71

Coach   So you said you want to telephone John. When will you do this?

Coachee   Next week sometime.

Coach   When exactly?

Coachee   Not sure yet. It depends on my schedule.

Coach   How does it depend on your schedule?

Coachee   OK, you're right. I need to make a commitment; I need to manage time better; I need to make a plan … you're right. So, I'll send an email and propose 4 o'clock our time on Tuesday. How does that sound?

Coach   How does it sound to you?

Coachee   It sounds good.

(View obstacles)

John's boss is identified as a potential obstacle. The solution is to ask the line manager of the coachee to contact John's boss to discuss the problem if the coachee and John cannot solve the problem themselves.

🔊 TRACK 72

Coach   So, is there anything that can stop you solving this problem with a telephone call?

Coachee   No, not really. I'm committed to doing it. I think John will be open and agree to lower objectives for our networking – and that should mean he'll ask for less information. Maybe the only problem could be his boss, if he keeps pressuring John for information.

Coach   OK. And what's a way around this?

Coachee   Hmm, tricky. He's not an easy guy. Very hierarchical. It's really not so easy for me to get to talk to him.

Coach   Would it be useful for your line manager to talk to him?

Coachee   Yes, I think that could be useful. If she does it informally, just a phone call and a general discussion, I think this could really help.

Coach   Good, when should she do this?

Coachee   I think we should keep it as a back up.
Let me talk to John first and then ...

(*Evaluate progress*)
The coachee enjoyed the questioning style of the
coach.

🎧 **TRACK 73**

Coach   So how do you feel about the session today?
Coachee   Very useful again. Good questions. Good
solution. And I think the more we talk, the more
I see time management is still a real issue I have
to deal with. I need to think about my planning
processes and prioritise and clarify objectives with
people ... or else work is going to be very difficult.
Coach   That sounds interesting. Maybe we can
come back to this at the start of the next session.
And the coaching style I was and am using? Any
comments?
Coachee   I like the questions. It keeps it open.
You're not telling me what to do. It makes me think.
It makes me see new parts of myself. So, good, very
good. I enjoyed it.